Prospecting Secrets

by

Jon Mason

CHOICE
PRESS

Choice Press LLC
15954 Jackson Creek Pkwy, Suite B, Box 501,
Monument CO, 80132

choice-press.com

Cover design by Akihiro Nakayama
and Rare Blue Moon Marketing

Set in Georgia & Satoshi fonts
Printed in the United States of America.

ISBN 979-8-9926998-5-2

For my family...

and future legacy

CONTENTS

FOREWORD

I first met Jon Mason in March of 2009 through his brother Dean, who got on the phone with me and said, "If you think you're impressed with me, you'll be very impressed with my brother."

Within a few minutes, I called Jon and asked him to come visit us in LA. He flew out immediately. I spent the whole time with him in LA at an event that we had at the Bonaventure Hotel. It was as if we had known each other for 10 years. Six months later, we started PHP agency. Jon spearheaded our East Coast operations, starting with Florida and expanding into Fort Lauderdale, Miami, Orlando, and Jacksonville.

What separates Jon above the average is he's very consultative. He's always asking questions and being curious. Where the average person needs to ask 7-10 questions to make a decision, Jon will be able to in just 3-4. He's extremely charming, charismatic, fun to be around, and great with people.

Prospecting Secrets is a timely book for today's entrepreneurs because it helps old school prospectors learn modern techniques (DM texting, LinkedIn, etc.), while it also helps younger prospectors learn the old school techniques of face-to-face interactions. Most people nowadays are afraid of talking to people in person. Technology is also rapidly changing. So, in a time like today, it's very important to know how to do both.

I've seen Jon prospect numbers of times. He will literally get up at a restaurant and go talk to somebody and get their number! On trips, I've seen him cold start a conversation with a stranger and by the time they're done, he's made the individual feel very comfortable with sharing their contact infor-mation. It's a tremendous skill. I've also seen Jon train hundreds of thousands of people over the last 16 years on stage.

On stage, Jon knows how to add value but also how to interact with the crowd and have fun. He would always come out to the song, "Put Your Hands Up in the Air" by Danzel. It's his main song. Jon and

I have been on stage together many times. One specific time, I played 'Doc' from "Back to the Future" while Jon played Marty McFly. Those videos are out there somewhere – hoping nobody sees them!

When I first met Jon, I wanted to make sure I could trust him to run our East Coast operation. So, I flew out to spend time with him and his family. I met his dad and his mom, and we stayed up till about three in the morning watching Danny Gans and Jon's old break-dancing Michael Jackson videos. The more I spent time with him and his family, traveling the world, sharing Christmases with our families together, the clearer it became to me that he was and is a man of great family values, of strength, reliability, and dependability.

Jon is a man of character.

~Patrick Bet-David,

Founder of Valuetainment and PBD Podcast

Chapter 1

The Prospector's Edge

The Four-Foot Eleven

Millionaire

In 2018, I met a 25-year veteran of the insurance business. He made close to $4,000,000 per year and had a large sales team. I asked him, "How much premium does your number one guy write per year?"

He said, "My top guy writes close to $5,000,000 a year in premium."

In the life insurance world, for one person to do that is a big and respectable number. Only the top

1% of insurance agents in the country can. I asked my friend, "What is that guy's secret?"

He looked at me with a smile. He told me that everyone always asks him the same question. He then asked me: "What do you think my guy looks like?"

My response was based on the typical stereotype of what most people envision of a successful salesperson.

"I'll guess that he is six feet tall, muscular, wears custom suits with Ferragamo shoes, has nice hair, cuff links on his shirt, and literally looks like a fitness model."

My friend smiled even wider and laughed humorously. He said, "Jon, my top sales guy is four-foot eleven, has big ears, a big nose, and walks with a little bit of a wobble!"

I was blown away by his response! I asked again, "Well, then what the hell is his secret?"

He said, "Jon, I asked him the same question over and over again. Every time I ask him, he gives me the same answer. He told me that when he was in high school, **he had to ask eighty-six girls to prom before one said YES.** Do you really think this business is hard?"

I learned one of the most important lessons of my career in that moment. It does not matter:

- How talented you are

- How you look

- Where you come from

- Your education level

- Your prior success of failures

All your success comes down to is your willingness and ability to PROSPECT!

Why Most People Fail in Sales

Why do so many people in sales or business fail within their first few years? Is it because they are not great closers? Is it because they don't have a quality product?

1. The Prospector's Edge

After being an entrepreneur for over twenty years, making every mistake in the book to now helping companies scale to the billion dollar plus mark, the common denominator I've seen that makes or breaks a career is the ability to generate NEW business. We call that prospecting.

Over the years, I've heard business owners and sales reps complain about how:

"The leads are bad..."

"The leads are expensive..."

"I need to generate more business..."

"The market is not doing well..."

"Business is slow because we are not in season yet..."

"We are waiting to see what the government votes on..."

The list goes on and on. None of those excuses produce results. All they do is justify a lack of income or business. But what if there was **a way to**

generate nonstop leads without having to come out of pocket, or to spend any money at all, and still get results no matter what time of year it is?

There is. It's called your skill set and mindset of prospecting.

Finding or Closing

What is more important in sales, finding or closing?

Most salespeople are concerned about becoming the ultimate closer. Some of the best cult classics are based on it, from *The Wolf of Wall Street* to *Boiler Room*. Closers love quoting the famous line, "Put that coffee down... coffee's for closers only."

But let me ask you, **who are you closing if you don't have anyone to close?** You can be the best closer in the world, but if you have no one to close to, it doesn't matter. You can have the best food, the best solar, the best real estate, the best insurance product... BUT, if you do not have a steady inflow of *prospects*, closing skills go to waste. Your closing ratio only matters if you have more reps under your belt.

Becoming a **Professional Prospector** is the secret sauce to building any business, sales team, and solid income stream.

The NFL Club:

No Friends Left, No Family Left,

No Funds Left

After college, I was looking for my dream lifestyle. I knew that the 9-to-5 life was not for me. I wanted to be able to set my family up financially and a typical salary would not do that.

I remember Jim Rohn once said, "A salary may pay the bills, but profits create a fortune." He also said, "Profits are better than wages."

That's what I wanted! To design a life! I was young, ambitious, energetic, and completely wet behind the ears. I had zero to no sales skills. I was a typical type-A personality that thought my "looks and talent" would make me a millionaire.

As I started to talk to my friends and family, I was met with pure resistance. No one took me seriously. I came from the entertainment industry as a breakdancer and entertainer. And now I was working on becoming a financial professional in the insurance industry.

Going from *breakdance to finance* with no sales skill is a recipe for disaster. I was becoming a part of the NFL club. What's the NFL club?

No friends left, no family left, no funds left, and no fun left!

I was overzealous, with no system to back it up.

Over time, I started reading books on sales, attending conferences, and watching sales and closing videos. Eventually, I got pretty good at closing. The only challenge was my income was not growing as fast as I wanted. Then, I realized something, "If I had more people to close, my income would grow."

My challenge was not closing, it was *FINDING*.

I needed a system that I could utilize to build my business while not scaring away my friends, family, and inner circle. That's when I started to develop specific language and behaviors to **attract the right prospects** and **increase my income**. I knew that there were specific steps to take, no matter what industry, which would increase my prospecting numbers. I just needed the secret formula.

If you own a restaurant, imagine suddenly doubling the number of people that come into your restaurant. If you are in health insurance or life insurance, imagine immediately doubling your income without having to spend 20-30% of your income on leads. If you are in network marketing, imagine growing your business without having to be cast into the NFL club.

The secrets that I learned, through trial and error, failure and success, are now being delivered to you in this very book. This book is the roadmap I wish I'd had when I first started.

Universal Relevance:

Salespeople, Realtors,

Agents, & Entrepreneurs

Whatever industry you're in, whether it's solar, insurance, network marketing, real estate, door to door, retail, medical device or pharmaceutical sales, this book will help you. If you are in any type of business at all, and your concern is to generate more business, *this book is exactly what you need.*

This book is designed to give you different formulas that you can apply instantly for yourself and your team to increase revenue and develop a predictable system for generating consistent results. It will help you to:

- Generate a steady flow of new leads and prospects.

- Reignite your business after you've plateaued.

Consistent prospecting allows you to live by design and not live by default. Prospecting allows you to control your income and live your dream lifestyle. Ask yourself this:

Who do I have to become to make my dreams a reality?

When I was first starting out in insurance, I moved from South Florida to Jacksonville. I didn't have enough money to rent my own place, so my buddy Tommy let me stay in his empty spare bedroom. I slept on a ten-year-old spring mattress on the floor. There was no furniture beyond an old-fashioned fat-backed TV. My car was my closet! Picture all of my suits hanging from the safety handles at the windows...

1. The Prospector's Edge

I was paying for an office in South Florida while also expanding into this new territory. I was taking a big risk, and I was not financially secure. I had to develop certain skill sets to become a successful player in my firm.

In my industry, there were people that were doing better than me. They were winning, and I wasn't *yet*. I had to figure out *why*. What were the successful ones doing that I was not?

I realized the answer: **Success is up to me**.

I was not prospecting enough. I made the decision to go on a prospecting blitz, increasing my number of qualified appointments. That mindset shift led to increased activity, which honed my skill set and grew our team into the top office in the country.

It can be very easy to fall into the victim mindset when things are not going your way. Rather, a *solution mindset* will not only build your character but will fix your situation. You can take immediate action and prospect your way out.

1. The Prospector's Edge

Remember this:

"If it's meant to be, it's up to me!"

The 4 Prospecting Markets

Part 1 of this book is about you. This first chapter shows you why you do what you do. **The second chapter** will teach you the psychology of prospecting, what works and what doesn't. **The third chapter** is about prospecting to recruit and retain a winning sales team.

Part 2 of this book is about the four main types of Prospecting Markets:

- Warm market
- Referral market
- Social Media
- Cold market

Part 3 of this book teaches you **how to follow-up**, the **daily habits/mindsets** to follow, and offers some **case-by-case prospecting scenarios**. You can also check the Appendix section of this book for **scripts, templates,** and **scheduling examples**.

Most importantly, this book will give you a system you can stick to, no matter what your experience, background, or industry. Whether you're in sales, building a team, or launching a business, this book will help you do the one thing that always leads to income:

Finding the people.

Conclusion

Your takeaway from this first chapter is *keep your main thing the main thing.* The main thing is solving the problem. Do not fixate on the problem. Rather, engage yourself emotionally with the *solution* to the problem. The solution to the problem is **PROSPECTING!**

Chapter 2

The Psychology of Prospecting

Lion in the Zoo

or Lion in the Jungle

A lion that lives at the zoo relies on others to feed him. It waits around all day for the zookeeper to come with its meal. If the zookeeper does not come, the lion does not eat. Over time, the lion loses its hunger-factor and settles for the basic meal that the zookeeper gives it.

Meanwhile, the lion in the jungle must hunt to survive. No one is coming to feed it. If the lion does not hunt, it does not eat. **You have to determine what type of lion you will be.**

I have seen so many people fail in business because they only rely on their company or manager to feed them leads. Leads can be expensive. What if the leads are not good? How big is your overhead if you are the one *feeding* your team with leads?

Buying leads can be a great way to make money, but if you can learn how to self-generate (aka *hunt for*) leads, then, like the lion in the jungle, you will never go hungry.

Let's say you are a server at a restaurant, or you sell gym memberships, or you sell cars. Are you a professional order taker waiting for people to come to you? Or are you going to hunt and increase your income for a better life?

For example, if you're a server in the restaurant business, why not make a list of 25 people and invite them to come and eat at your restaurant? Here's why you should:

- People have to eat anyways.

- The owner will give you better shifts, as you are generating business for the restaurant.

- You'll get better tips!

You have to get out from behind the desk and find the people! As the saying goes, *you have to see's the people to seize the people.*

Prospecting is a skill. Understanding the psychology of prospecting will increase your results.

Why We Fear Prospecting

(and How Ego Sabotages Success)

Why are we afraid to prospect? Wouldn't it be amazing if everyone we spoke to about our product, company, or service ended up buying from us or working with us? That's not the reality.

2. The Psychology of Prospecting

If a professional baseball player, who gets paid millions of dollars a year, who strikes out seven out of ten times, can still make the Hall of Fame, what makes you think you need *everyone* to say yes to you to become successful? The purpose of prospecting is to give yourself more swings at bat.

Not everyone you talk to has to become your client. **Our EGO is what is preventing us from achieving success**.

The reason why we don't prospect is because we're afraid of being embarrassed and rejected. When we are prospecting, and we get a *NO*, we internalize that. We feel rejected. We feel the prospect said *NO* to us because we are bad people or are not worthy of being liked.

In reality, the prospect saying *NO* had very little to do with our integrity as a person, and more with our skill set and mindset. The best part is, BOTH of those can be worked on. Learn how to turn *rejection* into *redirection*.

There's No Such Thing as

a Bad Conversation

There's no such thing as a bad conversation. There is only a *great* conversation or a *funny* conversation.

You have to realize that, just like the baseball player, even three hits out of ten doesn't mean those hits were home runs. Just because you exchanged information with a prospect, doesn't necessarily mean that it's going to lead to a sale.

So, a *great* conversation is when someone says *YES* and then:

They show up to your event.

They get started with your product.

They get started with your business.

They refer clients to you.

You can tell your skill is getting better when more people than not are saying *yes* and are following through.

A *funny* conversation is when someone says *NO* or an opportunity is declined. The funny part is, most people never actually use the word *NO!*

Rather, they sound like farm animals. They say things such as, "Nah", "Uh uh" or "Mm mm". These are typical knee jerk reactions from people that do not know how to properly communicate.

Sometimes it can be even more funny! Sometimes you get the prospect's number, invite them to your office to look at an opportunity, and suddenly you get the LinkedIn / Chat GPT response:

"Thank you for the opportunity. After careful consideration..."

Or you get the spousal response: "After speaking with my spouse...."

The interesting part is that most people turn down an opportunity or invitation without fully understanding what they are saying *NO* to. They are basing your approach on prior approaches and situations they have experienced.

By telling yourself these are funny conversations, it changes the narrative from discouragement to encouragement. The narrative changes your mindset. Your mindset changes your reality.

Rejection is Feedback, Not Failure

Let me be clear: rejection is not personal. Rejection is just a *redirection* to find a different approach. It's feedback. So, ask yourself, what is a lesson I can learn from this conversation or interaction?

Do I have to work on my approach?

Do I have to work on my scripts?

Do I have to get better at asking questions?

Where can I improve?

This goes back to the question you have to ask yourself, "Who do I have to become?"

Your mindset needs to be, "This person just said no to the best opportunity in their life. This person just said no to a life-changing opportunity. That's funny to me!"

Detached vs. Non-Attached:

Power vs. Force

I've heard finance gurus talk about how, "You have to be detached from the outcome."

Well, they are partially correct.

Detachment is derived from anger, frustration, and bitterness. It comes from an *I'll show you* and *I'll prove you wrong* mindset. On the **Power vs. Force chart by David Hawkins**, this stems from a lower personality vibration, the force side. In contrast, non-attachment is forgiveness. It allows you to operate without being attached to the outcome at all.

Non-attachment is being emotionally resilient. There is no need to justify, validate, explain, or over talk. You do not react. You just stay in the flow. The Ego is at peace. It is this mindset that lets you *prospect with relaxed intensity*, never desperate. You are not chasing. You are showing up confidently non-attached to the outcome.

Power Vs. Force Chart		
700+	Enlightenment	Higher Frequency · Expansive
600	Peace	
540	Joy	
500	Love	
400	Reason	
350	Acceptance	
310	Willingness	
250	Neutrality	
200	Courage	
175	Pride	
150	Anger	
125	Desire	
100	Fear	
75	Grief	
50	Apathy	Lower Frequency · Destructive
30	Guilt	
20	Shame	

From David Hawkin's *Power vs Force*

Here's a prospecting secret: Make sure you're acting from courage. Courage is the starting point of all positive energy. This can be seen as neutral (non-attached) or positive (high rate of vibration). In contrast, people that are complainers, blamers, and of victim-mentality are negative. They come from a low rate of vibration. You want to do your best to stay away from the low-vibration complainers.

Prospecting is also Negotiating

Non-attached also means the willingness to walk away.

The strongest form of negotiation is the willingness to walk away and never look back. If the prospect is not a fit for your service or product, you have to be willing to walk away knowing that there are other people that genuinely need you and your product in their life.

Fear of Success

& Prospecting Avoidance

I wasn't born into money.

I grew up watching my family struggle financially. My father had been a schoolteacher for decades. He always had a side hustle to make sure the family had what it needed. We were a typical middle American family, which developed a certain set of false beliefs in me about money, life, and business. I used to think that making money was hard. I saw my parents make money and lose it. I saw this pattern over and over again. Over time, I formulated a belief that my family was not supposed to have money because *every time we saw a little, it vanished.*

Self-sabotage happens when people are afraid of success. The reason that they're afraid of success is because they've been telling themselves this one story their entire life: They tell themselves they're not worthy, they don't deserve it, they're not good enough...

Then, if they were to ever become financially successful, it would mean **contradicting** everything they've been telling themselves. So, they avoid prospecting to avoid even the *possibility* of success. Their fear paralyzes them. They fail to prospect. In fact, prospect avoidance is their only way to control their outcome. Where does this mindset come from?

Maybe you grew up in a household where your parents said, "You can't do it. You're never going to make it. You don't deserve to go." Or maybe they said things like:

"We don't come from money."

"We're not that type of people."

"Money doesn't grow on trees."

"Rich people are greedy!"

You can respond to this by saying:

"Yeah, you're right...",

Or you can say:

"No, **I am successful**. I am letting go of my past and creating my future."

The fear of success will lead to prospecting avoidance. The past is the past. It's behind you for a reason. Leave it there.

Fear of Failure

There's a difference between failing and making a mistake. Most of us have grown up in a society where we are taught that making mistakes are bad. The reality is, making mistakes is the *best way to learn*. Making a mistake means you've acted from a high vibration of **courage** to take action, whether the outcome was successful or not.

The fastest way to learn and master your craft is to **make mistakes faster than your competition**. Getting past and letting go of the fear of failure starts with understanding what failure is. In prospecting, it's simple:

You can only fail when you stop prospecting.

You are allowed to make mistakes and learn from them. As long as you don't stop prospecting, you cannot fail. You no longer have to fear failure when you make a commitment to *consistently* act from courage, to *consistently* prospect.

Self-Worth and Identity:

Ferrari Energy Before Ferrari Income

The greater your self-esteem, the more successfully you'll prospect. Learn to work harder on yourself than you do at your job. The more valuable you become to the marketplace, the more invaluable you are. The more invaluable you are, the more your self-esteem will increase.

The fact is, the way you view yourself is the way others will view you. Other people can feel your energy and vibration. Many people in sales have this issue. They try to mask their low self-esteem by purchasing high-end material items:

Fancy cars, fancy clothes, and expensive jewelry will not make you feel better about yourself.

Yes, wearing a nice watch may help you start more conversations, but it will not change your low self-esteem. In fact, when you realize that your emotional state has not changed and your material item was a cover up for that low self-esteem, it may make you feel worse.

It's ok to buy nice things, especially if it helps with marketing or building up your image, but do not expect it to solve all your problems.

The secret is you have to believe in yourself before others will believe in you.

In 2016, I was operating from low confidence and low self-esteem. My business was stable but not aggressively growing. To mask my low self-esteem, I thought, "What if I buy a Ferrari? A Ferrari is a symbol of success. It'll help me to market my business and make me feel good about myself."

I was wrong. Later, I knew I was worthy of the Ferrari when I *didn't need* the Ferrari.

Be Childlike

There is a difference between being childlike and childish.

Childish is immature and unprofessional. The odds will be against you attracting qualified prospects if you act that way. However, acting childlike means loose, playful, relaxed, and high energy. Two points here.

First, sometimes we lose the fun in our business. Prospecting can be frustrating when we don't get results. Well, perhaps your energy is too low, or you are too serious and not relatable. Take a moment to check your energy and make sure you are finding the fun in the process. The fun is contagious!

Second, notice how small kids act when they are learning to walk: They keep falling down, and without thinking twice, they get back up. It's instinct to get back up. The challenge is that, over time, as we get older, we listen to a negative voice in our ear and get discouraged too easily.

We prospect and are instantly faced with resistance and start to doubt ourselves. When you realize, like the child falling, it's part of the process. The secret is to develop your mindset of getting back up no matter what.

Conclusion

The two things you can control are your **mindset** and your **skill set**. It is up to you to put in the work on those two things. **Remember, you only fail when you quit – so, keep on prospecting!**

Chapter 3

The Psychology of Recruiting

Prospecting to Recruit

Find out what the prospect is unhappy with and how you can be the solution. That's their pain point. Successful prospectors know what questions to ask to discover those pain points and to uncover the solutions.

In sales, you get paid to solve meaningful problems. The more problems that you solve, the more money you make. The more people you have to *help you* solve those problems, the more money you make *exponentially*!

There's two ways you can make money. There's **active** income and **passive** income.

Active income comes from all the work that you personally do. How many prospects and appointments can you get in one day or one week by yourself?

Passive income comes from all the work that's done for you. Passive income can come from recruiting and developing a sales force. The better you train your sales force, the more passive income you're making. If you had twenty sales reps on your team, how many prospects and appointments could *all of you* set in one day or in one week?

Wouldn't it make more sense to have that leverage and scalability?

That's why you recruit.

The secret to recruiting is simple: Find out what the prospect is unhappy with, and push on the pain points.

Your Ideal Recruit

It doesn't matter what industry you're in, if you're looking to build a sales team, you're looking for self-motivated, coachable, energetic, and competitive people.

If you have those qualities already, then you are exactly who you are looking for. If you're a high energy person, you're probably going to connect with people that are highly energetic. If you're more introverted, you probably will attract more people that are introverted. This is how *you* duplicate *you*. Remember this, **people like people who are like themselves**, but opposites are needed to support weaknesses and blind spots.

You don't want to limit yourself to duplicating your current self. You have weaknesses and shortcomings, so your goal in recruiting should be to **find people whose strengths match your weaknesses**.

If you're an introvert, you'll need an extrovert in your business and vice versa. Henry Ford wasn't the smartest person, so he recruited the best people around him to be smart *for him*.

Lead Channels for Recruiting

There are two channels for recruiting:

Channel 1: People can reach out to you.

Channel 2: You can reach out to people.

How you prospect to recruit is up to you, as long as you're prospecting. You can use recruiting websites, and CRM systems. You can buy leads, host live events. There's a broad array of prospecting options available.

Whatever option you choose, it's important to remember that great salespeople can come from anywhere. I've met great salespeople that were servers at a restaurant, or bartenders at a big club. They worked in a job that gave them face-to-face time with other people. Most people are overworked, underpaid, undervalued, overeducated, and overlooked.

Recent findings indicate that around half of working adults in the U.S. are dissatisfied with their current job, especially their pay and upward mobility, and over 50% are actively seeking or considering new job opportunities, often motivated by higher compensation[1].

Some people just need an opportunity. As a prospector, **it is your responsibility to offer that opportunity**.

Always be Recruiting

What you think about, you bring about.

---

[1] Pew Research Center, How Americans View Their Jobs, December 12, 2024, https://www.pewresearch.org/social-trends/2024/12/10/job-satisfaction/.

What you focus on expands. When you become intentional and focused on recruiting, you attract high volume, higher caliber people.

You should be prospecting all the time. It needs to be on your mind all the time. If you are in the teambuilding business and you feel stuck or frustrated, just remember, you want to hang out with **RITA** as much as possible!

Do you know who RITA is?

Recruiting Is The Answer!

Become a professional talent scout. The best sports teams have the best recruiters. The best companies have the best recruiters. But what makes them the best is, **they first know how to find**. They find a way to find the best talent. They have mastered the secrets of discovering hidden talent. That is your role as a prospector.

Your role is to prospect people's untapped hidden talent, to recruit them, and to develop them on your platform. That's how you build a winning team.

The Psychology of Recruiting

When you are prospecting, the potential new recruit is asking themselves several questions:

- If I work with you, will I have what you have?

- If I work with you, will you teach me what you know?

- If I work with you, will my life improve?

- What track record do you have?

- If you don't have a track record, can you introduce me to someone that does?

- I want to change the quality of my life, so if I work with you, what does that look like?

These are all questions that a prospect is asking that you need to be ready to answer.

Your language and attitude helps to control the narrative. Understanding a basic recruiting flow will help increase your results. There are three basic maneuvers you want to implement:

- **Take it away**. Don't make it too easy.

  Everybody wants what they can't have. Competitors love a challenge. More than a challenge, people love the feeling of overcoming obstacles. By adding a simple takeaway phrase, such as:

  "This may not be for you..."

  "There's an approval process..."

  "Let me see what I can do..."

  These simple phrases will help add value to your product or service.

- **Set up the next conversation.**

  The best prospector knows how to build long-term relationships. People hate to be sold, but they love to buy. By building a relationship with your prospect, it gives them a chance to feel empowered and the ability to purchase or get started with you.

Having multiple conversations and sit-downs with your prospect will naturally build that relationship over time. This builds trust and certainty.

- **Be ready to leverage leadership.**

  You don't have to have the answers for everything, especially if you're new. But you do need to become resourceful and able to *find the people that do*.

  No matter what industry you're in, you should have access to experienced sales reps and leadership that can speak to your prospects on your behalf.

The Catch-All Recruiting Tool:

An Invitation is not a Presentation

A mistake that I see sales professionals make is they present too much, too soon, too fast. Successful prospectors keep people curious.

Here's a simple conversational script and flow that works. It even works for more than just prospecting to recruit. Remember: Prospecting is prospecting. Sales is sales. Once you know how to prospect for one thing, you can prospect for anything.

These are four basic questions to open a conversation and then close with four simple words: **If I, will you**.

I learned this technique from Eric Worre's *Go Pro*, and it's worked for me every time. Eric's book was written for Network Marketing, but in my opinion, it is a business book that should be studied by all business professionals. Here's how this works:

Prospect to Recruit Script

Question 1: *What kind of work are you in?*

Question 2: *How long have you been there for?*

Question 3: *Would you be open to a different career if it made sense? Or, something on the side if it made sense?* (part-time or full-time depending on your opportunity)

Question 4: *So, you do keep your options open?* (say this more as a statement rather than a question)

Prospect to Sell Script

(Example: Insurance)

Question 1: *Who is currently helping you with your insurance and retirement?*

Question 2: *How long have you used them for?*

Question 3: *Are you 100% content or would you be open to possibly saving more money, paying less in taxes, and speeding up your retirement?*

Question 4: *So, you are open to a conversation?* (say this like it's already true)

Usually at this point, for either script, people will have questions. Be careful with your answers. No matter your industry, if you give too much away too soon, there's no reason for them to meet with you again. You want to give them enough information to educate them *and excite them for more.* There's a simple phrase that will educate the prospect, hold them accountable, and keep them curious.

If I, will you

- *"Here's what I'd like to do. I'd like to send you some information ahead of time for you to review. If I send you this [information on your offer], will you read it?"*

Next, confirm your follow-up

- *"Great, when can you read that by?"* (or watch that by if it's a video)
  - Next, let them confirm a time
- *"Perfect, so we will reconnect at [time] and have another conversation. Sounds fair?"*

This technique takes time to master. Keep in mind, you want to speak slowly while having confidence in your tone and confidence in your questions. You want to ask each question with the belief that you have the best product and service in the marketplace.

Remember, *silence is golden*. Do not say too much.

The Mindset of Recruiting

There're three outcomes of recruiting:

- **Recruit to recruit**

  This means that you're just trying to hit a number or a quota, but you really have no intention of working with people.

- **Recruit to sell**

  This means you'll work with people a little bit, and make some money with them, but you are not invested in developing them or building a long-term relationship.

- **Recruit to build**

This means you're invested in their success, and your plan is to help develop them and build a long-term relationship.

Think about it like this:

You can date somebody, but if you break up with them, it doesn't matter. You can date someone and marry them, but that doesn't matter if you don't *stay married*. The purpose of dating is to get married, and the purpose of marriage is to stay married.

It's about the long term: Have kids, and then grandkids, and teach them your values and principles. The way you can tell if you were a good parent is not just by your kids, but how your grandkids are raised.

It's the same thing in business.

If you are in the recruiting business, what values and principles are you teaching your new agents, your new reps, your new distributors? Are they teaching *their* new reps, *their* new distributors, what you taught them?

You can tell how good of a trainer you are by your team's success. If your team is not at the level you want them to be, it means you haven't trained them well enough.

Retaining Your Recruits

Remember this formula: **retention = more prospects.**

Why?

If you don't take care of your people, someone else will. ~Patrick Bet-David.

Keeping your top performers motivated is a science. First, find out what motivates your top salespeople. A great leader understands that different people are motivated by different things. Some are motivated by trips, some are motivated by material items, while others are motivated just by simple recognition.

For example, if your top performer is motivated by trips and travel, and you're running a contest recognizing them with a pair of shoes, you may not get the most out of them. But if your top performer told you over lunch that it's their dream to go to the Maldives, and you run a contest with a dream trip to the Maldives as the *top prize*, the chances are your top performer will go **above and beyond**.

And because your top performer raised the bar for everyone else, your top 80% of performers will also up their game because the lead horse sets the pace.

The secret is: **Find out what makes your top performers tick.**

Environment Matters

Over the years, I've found success building multiple office environments. Human nature shows that people will run through walls for recognition. For example, when we gave awards to our top performers, we invited friends and family that were not a part of our company to witness their friend or family member be recognized publicly. I would also set up dinners which friends and family members could attend.

While I was in Jacksonville, I would host trainings in my office on Tuesday evenings. After training, the office and I would drive two blocks away to a Dave & Buster's to have some food and fun. We also invited people that were not with the company to join us, just to hang out.

This environment allowed us to let our guard down and enjoy each other's company.

Prospecting people into a fun, high-energy environment will put the odds in your favor for that prospect to start working with you. Top performers love competition. Great leaders know how to stir competition amongst peers while also aligning them towards a team goal.

You have to realize, top performers get bored easily. Having daily, weekly, monthly, quarterly, and annual competitions and contests are a great way to keep top performers engaged while discovering and training new talent. Just like in a relationship, you have to keep it exciting!

Recruit Through Recognition

If you're taking your team to a Ferragamo store to buy them shoes, there will be other people in the store that will *see you* taking care of *your team*. Your team, and other people, will most likely take pictures and post about this on social media. That's going to create a buzz. Three things will then happen:

1) People that are *watching* are going to want to be a part of it.

2) People that are *working* with you but didn't win are going to be more motivated to win the contest next time.

3) You will have higher retention because the people that are being recognized feel seen and appreciated.

Taking care of your team is retaining your team, and that's also creating more prospecting opportunities. How?

Let's say you run an office. If a prospect comes to your office, and your office is buzzing with high energy, fun, and enthusiasm, the prospect is going to be more enticed to work with you. They see the retention of your business and the fun environment you've created.

Consider the opposite of this:

Let's say you run an office. What if a prospect comes to your office, and your office is empty? Or, let's say that no one who's there is happy or having fun? If this happens, your prospect or recruit will turn around and walk out the door and you'll never see them again.

Your Values Attract Valuable Recruits

The way you live your life is going to attract or repel potential prospects. This includes:

- Books you read

- Meetings you attend

- Associations you have

- Practicing core values

- Keeping your word

- Coming through

If you live a life of integrity, your recruits will usually have integrity. A team with integrity is long-lasting, effective, respected, and successful. Practice what you preach!

Conclusion

Always be recruiting.

Prospecting to recruit is about developing and building long-term relationships. Growing a sales-force takes time, patience, and consistency.

Action Steps

1. Create Your Recruiter's Playbook Write down the top five questions you'll ask every prospect to uncover their pain points. Practice using the "If I, will you?" technique with friends or team members until it feels natural. This gives you a consistent flow you can rely on, no matter who you're talking to.

2. Build Your Ideal Team Blueprint Make a two-column list: one side for your strengths and the other for your weaknesses. Then, define what kind of personalities and skills would balance you out. This helps you stop cloning yourself and start building a team that covers your blind spots.

3. Design a Recognition-Retention Plan

Ask your top reps what motivates them most: trips, gifts, recognition, or responsibility. Based on their answers, plan one high-impact recognition activity for next month that makes your culture visible and contagious. Retention builds recruiting momentum.

4. Audit Your Recruiting Environment

Walk into your office, Zoom, or event space like a new recruit seeing it for the first time. Is it buzzing with energy? Does it feel like a team you'd want to be part of? If not, list three changes you can make this week to raise the energy and improve first impressions.

PART II

Chapter 4

Warm Market Prospecting

From Breakdance to Finance:

Jon's Warm Market Reality

I was twenty-six when I first got into the insurance business. My brother introduced me to PBD in 2009. For the last decade before, all I knew was the entertainment industry, emceeing and dancing at weddings, bar mitzvahs, and corporate events.

I was literally transitioning from breakdancing to financing.

The only challenge was, I had zero credibility in the financial world. Imagine emceeing a bar mitzvah and then asking the family to do their life insurance and retirement planning. Let's just say that did not go over so well! I had no skill set, no sales training, and no experience.

So, when it was suggested that I start with my warm market to recruit and sell to, I thought it would never work. Then I realized something. Everyone that I loved, trusted, and cared about needed what I had. I also realized that they would be going to *somewhere or someone else* to get what I had to offer. Why not come to me if I could be a resource for them? I just had to figure out the formula to get in front of them without being the stereotypical salesperson.

Why Friends Don't Trust You (Yet)

Understand this: the people that know you are not always going to give you their business right away. You are new! They know that! It's really that simple. In fact, most people are expecting you to quit within the first six months. So, while you might be excited, and they might be excited for you, they still don't know if you're going to be around doing what you're doing past the six-month mark. Understand where they're coming from.

The insurance industry has an 89% turnover rate within the first three years.[1] For network marketers, at least 50% of recruits drop out within the first year, and 90–95% leave within five years.[2] For salespeople in general, the average turnover rate is 35% per year, roughly three times the general average.

So, you have to put yourself in your warm market's shoes. Think about it this way, if someone was brand new in the financial industry, would you trust that person with your life savings? Probably not. So, you really can't blame them if they don't buy from

---

[1] AgencyBloc, "Why 89 % of Insurance Agents Quit Within 3 Years," AgencyBloc Agent Management, https://www.agencybloc.com.
[2] Christensen, Scott. 2020. "The High Cost of Low MLM Representative Retention."

you just because you were friends for twenty years. However, they might trust you if you have the credibility established. How do you do that?

The Trust Timeline:

Negative, Neutral, Positive People

It does not matter whether you are in real estate, health insurance, life insurance, solar, or anything where you have a product to offer. The formula is the same. Your warm market is going to consist of 3 types of people:

1) Negative People

Negative people have nothing that you want. I've never met a negative successful person. People that are negative typically don't have any financial success. In contrast, the most successful people I know are *always* willing to help. They're positive. They point you in the right direction.

I'll say it again: I've never met a negative successful person.

2) Neutral People

There are some people that you approach that are neutral. Neutral people can care less, but they're not going to be negative. So, what's the advantage with approaching neutral people?

The advantage is that now they know what you do, and maybe you can be a resource to them in the future. They can be potential prospects in the future or refer prospects your way.

3) Positive People

Positive people are typically the most successful. They typically have the lifestyle and income that you want. They're the ideal person for your warm market.

Here's the thing, you get to choose who you want to hang around. For your warm market, you want someone who really has your back. You won't know who your positive people are until you reach out. A friend from high school does not mean they're gonna be supportive of you now.

So, a positive person in the past can become a negative person when you reach out to them again. It also means, a negative or neutral person in the past can become a positive person now.

Turn to page 33 to see the Power vs. Force Chart again. You'll see that:

Negative people are starting from shame, guilt, apathy, grief, fear, desire, anger and pride.

Neutral people start from courage.

Positive people start from willingness, acceptance, reason, love, joy, and peace.

How to Categorize and Segment

Your Warm Market List

Here are two simple steps to take to help you get in front of your Warm Market.

Step 1: Make the list

If they are in your phone, put them on the list. If they are in your social media, put them on the list.

Look at it this way, *if people are in your cell phone or a part of your social media contacts and you have no intention of ever speaking with them, why are they in your phone or social media circle?* The main reason for contacting people that you know is to let them know what it is that you do.

That's it!

Step 2: Contact them

Phone calls are always going to be your best approach as your tone and energy can be felt over the phone. In today's market, a properly written text message will also open up doors into your warm market. Do not expect everyone to respond to you right away.

It will take days to months to work through your warm market and start to see results.

The 3 Core Approaches

You have a few approaches you can take if you are prospecting your warm market to offer them a product or service:

You can be Direct, Indirect, or use the Leverage Approach.

The Direct Approach:

Car Sales: "Hey Mary, would you or anyone you know perhaps be in the market for a new car?"

Gym Membership: "Hey Mary, would you or anyone you know perhaps be in the market to look at joining a new gym?"

Medical devices: "Hey Mary, do you happen to know any doctors that you can connect me with?"

Real Estate: "Hey, Mary, do you happen to know anyone that would be looking to buy or sell a house?"

Solar: "Hey Mary, do you happen to know anyone that wants to save money on their energy bills?"

Health Insurance: "Hey Mary, do you happen to know anyone that wants to save money on their health insurance coverage?"

Life Insurance: "Hey Mary, do you happen to know anyone that wants to add long-term care to their plan?"

Restaurant: I would ask every server to put together a warm market list and ask the following:

"Hey, Mary! It's Jon, I just got a job serving at [XYZ Restaurant]. The food is amazing. I'd love for *you* to come in!"

If you own any business, have your staff do something like that. Remember, everything is sales! Whether it's barber shops or sub shops or insurance or solar, have your people get more people. Make this part of their onboarding process and recognize them when one of their warm market prospects moves forward with your product or service.

"Hey Mary, I wanted to reach out to you because I just took a position with..."

"Hey Mary, I wanted to reach out to you because..."

This even works if you are recruiting.

"Hey Mary, would you be open to making money on the side if it made sense?" or,

"Hey Mary, would you be open to making more income than you currently are? Something came across my plate that I feel you might be interested in."

"Mary" may not get started with the opportunity, but she sure knows a lot of people!

The Indirect Approach:

Car Sales: *"Hey Mary, I know you may not be looking for a car, but is there anyone that you know that may be looking to upgrade their vehicle?"*

Gym Membership: *"Hey Mary, I'm sure you love your gym, but we just upgraded our facility. Do you happen to know anyone that may be looking for a gym membership?"*

Life Insurance: *"Hey Mary, I'm sure you already have something in place, but do you happen to know anyone that perhaps wants to pay less on their coverage, or maybe wants to add long-term care to their plan?"*

Network Marketing: *"Hey Mary, I know what I do may not be for you, but is there someone that you can introduce me to..."*

The purpose of the Indirect Approach is the *takeaway mindset*. When you add the phrase *may not be for you*, people are now questioning, *"Why would it not be for me??"*

Remember, people want what they can't have.

So, what may have been a resistant prospect is now open to a conversation.

The Leverage Approach:

If you are brand new to an industry and have zero experience, how much credibility do you have? None! So, what do you do? You **LEVERAGE** someone who has the credibility!

Introduce your prospect to your mentor or trainer. You can say something like, *"Hey, I just got my insurance license. I'm in a broker program. I'm new and need your help. Could you hop on a training call with me and my broker so I can learn the words and get some experience under my belt?"*

Then, tell them about your mentor. Say something like, *"This is Jon Mason. He's worked in finance for 16 years. He's an expert in the industry."*

The leverage is someone else who has the experience and credibility leading the training.

The same goes for any industry you are in:

- If you are in health insurance, leverage your broker.

- If you are in real estate, leverage your broker.

- If you are in solar, leverage your sales leader.

Even if you have to split or share a commission, 50% of something is a lot better than 100% of nothing. Plus, you now get the experience, and your warm market receives quality information and perceives you as a serious professional. When you are new or learning something new, you want to learn as much as you can as fast as you can.

Leveraging credibility is one of the fastest ways to learn any industry you are in.

"When a man with experience meets a man with money, the man with the money leaves with experience and the man with experience leaves with the money" **– Warren Buffet**

Build your credibility by *providing* credibility. The mindset that you want to always have is this: Drop me in the desert, and I'll build.

Edifying

You want to give your leadership or trainer the power position in any prospecting situation. When you edify, you are setting aside your ego and putting your leadership on a pedestal. In a later chapter, I'll share with you a story of how I leveraged edification. A basic formula for edifying someone is **COP**.

Company (who they are in the company)

Office (what role they play in the office)

Personal (a personal story of how they've impacted their life)

For example, *"Hey Mary, I want you to meet Joe. He's a senior broker in the firm and top trainer in the office. I wouldn't be in the position I'm in without Joe's guidance and leadership. I'm very grateful for the time he has invested in me."*

You want to edify anyone and everyone every chance you get. Remember, it's okay to talk about people, even behind their back, if it's in a positive way.

Conclusion

The longer you stick with one thing, the more your warm market will take you seriously. Later in this book, we will discuss a follow-up program that works for your warm market.

Action Steps

1) **Build and Organize Your Warm Market List**

   Go through your phone contacts and social media connections and write down every name that comes to mind. Once you have your list, sort each person into one of three groups: negative, neutral, or positive. This will help you know who to contact first and what type of tone to use when you reach out.

2) **Choose the Right Approach for You**

Decide which of the three methods — Direct, Indirect, or Leverage — best matches your confidence level and current experience. Write out 5-10 custom messages using that method, and start reaching out right away. The sooner you act, the faster you gain confidence and results.

3) **Use Credibility to Build Credibility**

If you are still new in your business, do not try to act like an expert. Instead, lean on someone who is. Schedule a call with a mentor or experienced leader and invite a prospect to join you. Practice your edification script using the Company, Office, Personal formula so you can introduce your leader with confidence and respect.

4) **Track Your Progress and Stay Consistent**

Choose a simple way to track your outreach, whether it is a spreadsheet, journal, or contact list. Log every name, every conversation, and every follow-up. You are not trying to close everyone right away. You are showing up, proving your consistency, and building trust over time.

Chapter 5

Referral Prospecting Secrets

Why Referrals are the Highest ROI Leads

The challenge with most people is that when they work all the way through their warm market, they ask, "Now what?" Most sales reps fail because they cannot continue to get into new markets. Referrals are the *first* solution to this problem.

Here's a secret: Referrals are my FAVORITE type of prospects! When I was working in the entertainment industry, mainly in the Bar Mitzvah market, after every show two things would happen:

First, parents from different families would come up to me to give compliments of how great a time they had. They'd never seen a show like it and would go on to say that they have their own family events coming up. They wanted to see if we were available to perform at their event.

Second, the host of the event would come up to me and thank me, give a cash tip, and then PERSONALLY INTRODUCE me to some of their friends that were looking at having events in the future. That was literally the easiest NEW business I ever earned. Why?

IT was a REFERRAL!

When you learn to give Unreasonable Hospitality, go above and beyond "just your job", and follow through on your job duties to show a client that you are not just a transactional sales rep, but rather a genuine individual that values relationships and keeping your word. CURRENT CLIENTS are more than willing to open their rolodex to you and refer you to people that can benefit from your product or service.

One of the biggest challenges I see sales reps face is that they ask for referrals without having a relationship with their client, or they did not actually offer quality service. One way to overcome this is to *build deep-rooted relationships with your prospects and clients.* Put together a **KYC (Know Your Customer)** that lists celebrations, occasions, and their favorites.

"The key to a person's heart is an unexpected gift at an unexpected time." – Sean Connery

The littlest attention to detail can have the greatest impact. The more you know your clients and prospects, the more comfortable they will be with you.

You can use different types of data entry and CRM systems to capture information on your clients. If you want to add that extra touch, send out a form to all of your current clients or prospects that may not have done business with you yet. On that form you can have them list their:

5. Referrals

Full name

Mailing address

Contact info

Spouse's name and DOB

Children's names and DOB

Favorite food

Favorite restaurant

Favorite beverage/wine

Favorite sports team

Anniversary

Date of birth

Shoe size

Favorite color

Favorite snack

Favorite way to de-stress

Favorite music/band

Favorite movie

Favorite animal

If you want to practice filling in a chart of your own, turn to page 212 of this book. There's a handy template there for you!

- Make sure to set reminders for any occasions that arise regarding any of these. Use them as an excuse to reach out to your client or prospect.

Season is the Reason

In the United States, there's a holiday every month. There're multiple professional sports leagues in multiple places around the country. There's always a reason to contact your current clientele. This is called *Season is the Reason*; it's using current events, relevant situations, or holidays, etc. to start a conversation with someone.

This will be mentioned several times throughout the book, as it's a strategy that can be used for different formats. The outcome is always *to start a conversation.*

1) Make a list of ALL your current customers or clients

2) CALL them using the **Season is the Reason**

- "Hey Chris, did you see the game last night?"

- "Hey Pat, any travel plans for the summer?"

ASK, ASK, ASK

The other challenge I have seen is that most sales reps don't even ASK for a referral. Here are some gut-punching statistics: **91 %** of customers say they'd provide referrals, but only **11 %** of salespeople ask for them.[1] Meanwhile, Salespeople who actively seek referrals **earn 4–5×** more than those who don't.[2]

In the hustle, bustle, grind it out world of sales, most reps are focused on NEW accounts. Their interpretation of a NEW account is either buying a lead or randomly meeting someone.

In reality, a referral is the MOST POWERFUL NEW type of account you can get. Why?

If one of your clients refers you new business, and that referral ends up doing business with you, BOTH your current client and your NEW referral client most likely have some people in the same circle. The word of mouth will spread faster as you now have two people in the same market talking about you behind your back.

So, what will happen over time, because you did your part by doing a great job as well as building

[1] Zahradnik, Matthew. Referral Statistics: Why You Should Be Asking for Referrals. HubSpot, July 7, 2022. https://blog.hubspot.com/service/referral-statistics.
[2] Ibid.

a relationship, is your current clientele will ask you if it's okay to **pass your number to** people in their network.

At the SAME time, the referrals also have NEW networks that they will be introducing you to. So, realistically, you have NEW Prospects coming in ALL the time.

The Trust Transaction:

Reputation on the Line

Why would someone refer business to somebody if they didn't keep their word? If they kept their word, did a great job, and went above and beyond, you'll feel comfortable doing business with them again. If you're comfortable doing business with them again, you're more than happy to connect them with the right people.

People want to protect their rolodex. People want to protect their contacts, because every time they refer somebody to you, their reputation is on the line. The moment they connect you with their inner circle, their reputation is at stake. That's why establishing the relationship first is so important.

The Difference Between Referrals & Personal Introductions

A personal introduction is more powerful than a generic referral. What sounds better to you:

Referral: *"Jon, call Mike..."*

Personal Introduction: *"Jon, I would like to personally introduce you to Mike. Mike, Jon is an expert in the financial industry and has personally helped me and my family save on taxes and update our retirement plans to have more guaranteed income down the road. I know you may have someone you currently work with, but I feel a conversation with Jon will be worth your time."*

- How many current clients do you have that need a text or phone call from you?

- Who can you call right to see how they are doing?

When to Ask: Post-Delivery Moments

Right now!

Don't wait for your company to send out their survey email. **YOU have to take the initiative!** You are the one that has the relationship with the client. In any industry, the best time to ask for an introduction is after giving quality service.

Why? Because if you ask too soon, the client may feel that the attention is about you getting your next sale and not on them.

The purpose of ASKING for Referrals and Introductions AFTER the delivery of the product or service is to keep the attention focused on the current customer. Let them know you care about them and not just your next sale. People will be inclined to help you more when they know you care. John Maxwell said it best, "People don't care about how much you know until they know how much you care."

Here are some examples of when to ask for a referral, by industry. You can utilize the phrase, *"Is there anyone that you can personally introduce me to?"* or, *"Is there anyone that you can personally connect me with?"*

Insurance: When delivering the insurance policy.

Real Estate: After closing.

Solar: After installation.

Network Marketing: After the product or service has been delivered.

Car Sales: During the customer survey follow-up call.

Server: After dessert.

Gym Sales: After a training session.

CPA: After you've filed their taxes.

Can you ask for referrals or introductions sooner?

Yes! As long as you have a connection with the prospect or client and trust is established.

Strategic Partnerships

One day, I was at a Yankees game with PBD and the Valuetainment crew. One of Patrick's former Army sergeants, Felix, surprised Patrick there, and we started catching up on good old times. I've known Felix for almost ten years. He said that he just took a position as a financial advisor at a credit union. He said that he's trying to build up his new book of business. I asked him, "Well, how many strategic referral partnerships do you have set up?"

Surprised, he asked, "What do you mean?"

"Well, who's actually giving you business at the credit union?"

He said, "Oh, well the banker is."

"Who else?"

Again, he asked, "Well, what do you mean?"

"First off, the affluent market doesn't take their money to credit unions. They take it to other bigger institutions. Therefore, why would affluent people come to a credit union?"

"Because they want car loans."

I said, "Exactly! Are you the one that gives them out?"

"No...", he replied.

My response was: "So, who are the ones that do? Connect with them!"

I added: "Let's say I'm looking for a Lamborghini, or I'm looking for a bigger loan, I know credit unions typically have better rates. The guys that give out these loans are the ones that have the connection with the affluent market, which in turn is the market that you want to get into. Have you ever gone up to them and offered to take them out for coffee, or built a relationship with them?"

Felix said, "No, I haven't even thought of that!"

And he smiled at me and said, "As soon as I get home, I'm doing that."

I said, "Do you want to take it a step further? You and I are friends. I want you to text me every time you make that connection. And if you want to take it a step further than that, as soon as you get back on Monday, text me every day for the first two weeks to let me know how those conversations are going and what you have planned. When you're holding yourself accountable to getting a situation or a task done, you'll do it better, faster, and stronger because of that positive peer pressure."

Expanding Your Sphere of Influence

Ask yourself, what other industry can YOU send business to? The chances are THEY will be able to send business YOUR way!

Meaning, if you're in real estate, how many mortgage brokers can you send business to?

If you're in real estate, how many pest control people do you have in your referral network? Similarly, if you're in pest control, how many roofing, mortgage, real estate, people do you know?

You also want to develop spheres for yourself.

Meaning, what industries specifically do business with each other? In the financial industry, that's life insurance, estate planning, financial advisors, health and disability insurance, estate planning, accountants, and CPAs, just to name a few. Anything under the financial game plan is a strategic partnership.

Ask-to-Give Framework

A simple question you can ask a center of influence is this, "**Who can you connect me to?**"

5. Referrals

Or you can gently go up to them and say, "*Hey, Florence, I need your help. I'm looking to meet someone in (be specific), is there a way you can make that introduction?*"

When you ask your sphere of influence for help, it needs to be reciprocated. Never make it a one-way street. When you're dealing with business owners, or people that earn income from commission, and you're expecting to get referrals, *the best way to start getting referrals is to give referrals.*

Whenever I build a strategic partnership, the questions I ask are:

- "*How can I add value to you?*"

- "*Who is it that you are looking to meet?*"

- "*I come across all sorts of people, if I could make one introduction for you that would help your business, who would that be?*"

When it comes to strategic partnerships, it's more about giving than gaining. When you give, you're going to gain. Zig Ziglar, author of *Secrets of Closing the Sale*, said, "If you help enough people get where they have to go, you'll get where you have to go."

Think about it this way, the more people that you help connect with other people, the more connections you are going to receive.

Collaboration Prospecting:

Building Without Warm Leads

Expanding your market through collaboration can multiply your prospecting numbers. This is similar to asking for a strategic partnership. But this time, you're doing that without a referral to vouch for you. It is a simple process that requires daily commitment and consistency. It's the same process for whatever industry you're in:

5. Referrals

Step One: Go online and find everyone that's related to your sphere of industry that you would be able to send referrals to.

The reason is:

Collaboration is a two-way street. If you cannot send referrals either way, or don't ever plan to, the relationship will not work.

If you are in real estate, find every mortgage broker in your local area.

Step Two: Call them. If you cannot find their number, send them a PERSONALIZED direct message through social media, email, etc., similar to what you would say over the phone.

"Hey, Joe, this is John. The reason I'm calling you is because I'm a realtor in the local market. I was wondering if you are open to collaborating and sharing business."

Remember, this is not recruiting or selling. It's not a cold call. It's an invitation for collaboration.

Here's an even more concrete example. If you are in life insurance:

Step One: Make a list of everybody that's in health insurance, real estate, mortgage, P & C insurance, taxes, or anyone that you can also send referrals to.

Step Two: Call them. (Send them a personalized message elsewhere if you don't have their phone number)

"Hello, this is John. I'm in the life insurance sector. I was wondering if you're open to possibly seeing if we can collaborate and share business."

It does not matter what your industry is. The formula is the same across board. The secret is to take action and build relationships.

5. Referrals

Write the Referral Script for

Your Clients

When it comes to asking for a referral or introduction, some people may not know what to say. So, it's best if you write out the statement and have them authorize it. Then, they can send it out from their phone.

It's best if they do this in a group message.

An example of this would be:

"Hey Mary, I'm sitting here with my solar expert..." or, *"I'm sitting here with my insurance expert..."* or, *"I'm sitting here with my real estate expert..."*

Then you can finish this statement by saying,

"Do you have anyone that helps you handle... (solar, insurance, real estate)? If not, I would highly recommend a conversation with them!"

It's that simple.

Beneficiary Referrals:

A Natural Prompt

In some industries, such as insurance, there's going to be a beneficiary of that policy. Some companies, in the network marketing industry for example, allow you to pass on your business to a beneficiary.

If the person is single, they may put a sibling or relative as the primary beneficiary. If the client is married, for a personal policy they will most likely put their spouse as the primary beneficiary. The secret sauce is to ask about who will be their "contingent" beneficiaries.

My question is, "God forbid, what happens if something happens to both of you?"

A way to ask for a referral here can be like this,

"If something were to happen to you and your spouse, in whose hands would you place the responsibility of your children?"

Those new names are the contingent beneficiaries. You can call those beneficiaries and say:

"Hi Chris, this is Jon, your brother's insurance agent. He wanted me to reach out to you to let you know that you are a contingent beneficiary and to make sure you have my contact information. When your brother and I spoke, he had a policy in place but was missing [X,Y,Z]. He mentioned that you may be in the same situation. I was curious, do you know what type of plan you have?"

I've personally used this script for the majority of my career. It works! All you need to do is take this concept and *customize it to your industry.*

The Secret Sauce:

Specific Asks Get Specific Results

You want to be as specific as possible when seeking a referral or introduction. The more specific you are about what you're requesting, the more likely they are to connect you. Rather than just asking for an introduction, ask for a specific introduction.

For example, you can say something like, *"Joseph, do you have a best friend or family member right now that might be getting married? Well, the reason I'm asking is most couples want to review their finances before marriage, but they don't have anybody in their corner. I'd love the opportunity to earn their business by being their insurance advisor. Would you mind making a personal introduction for me?"*

That's how you ask. You ask specifically about what you're looking for.

Here's another example:

"Hey, Joe, do you know anyone that lost their job recently that might be looking for a different career, or is maybe just unhappy where they're at?"

If you're recruiting to your company, ask *"Do you know anybody looking for more income? Or someone that just left their job, looking for something different, or they're just bored?"*

Real Estate: *"Do you know anyone that just got married? Most new couples are looking to purchase a home."*

Have a list of specific questions to ask ready-to-go before you ask.

The more specific you are in your request, the more likely you are to get a result.

Create a Center of Influence

Having a mentor and a center of influence can open up doors for you. It is important to have a deep-rooted relationship with your mentor. Make a list of five people you would like to build a relationship with. Offer to take them to coffee or buy them a meal. Continue to do this once a quarter to strengthen the relationship.

Remember, your success in business will be determined by the books you read, the meetings you attend, and the associations you have. Choose your environment wisely.

Action Steps

1. Turn Clients into Connectors
Reach out to your current clients and check in with them, even if they already bought from you. Use the "season is the reason" to start a natural conversation. After a meaningful exchange, ask if they know anyone else who could benefit from what you do. Aim for a *personal introduction*, not just a name and number. If needed, write the referral message for them and have them send it in a group text.

2. Build a Strategic Referral Network
List five local professionals in industries that complement your own. If you are in real estate, think of mortgage brokers, insurance agents, and home inspectors. Reach out and invite them to coffee or a

quick phone call. Your offer should be simple and genuine: *"I'd love to see how we can share business and send referrals both ways."*

3. Ask Specifically and Intentionally

Before you ask for a referral, decide exactly what kind of person you're looking to connect with. Do not ask general questions like *"Do you know anyone?"* Instead, say something like, *"Do you know a couple who just got engaged?"* or *"Do you have a friend who recently left their job and might be open to something new?"* The clearer you ask, the stronger your results.

4. Strengthen Your Sphere of Influence

Pick five people you admire in your space or community and invite one of them to coffee this week. Your goal is not to pitch, but to build long-term relationships with mentors or connectors. Make a habit of reaching out quarterly and finding ways to add value to their life or business. These centers of influence will become some of your strongest sources of referrals over time.

Chapter 6

Social Media That Works

Your Social Media Is Your New Business Card

Think about it. The first thing someone is going to do, when they hear about you, is go to your social media account. Just like with a business card, you want to make the best first impression possible.

Prospecting in the social media market is not about making a post and just hoping someone responds to it. That's called being lazy and hoping to get lucky. Rather, it's about following specific protocols to consistently attract quality prospects.

Choosing the Right Platform

for Your Industry

There's a right platform(s) to use for the industry you're in. The thing is, this changes every several years or sooner. There are always new platforms coming out.

As of the writing of this book, the platforms to use are Instagram, X, Tik-Tok, LinkedIn, YouTube, and Facebook, to name a few. These change over time and for different reasons, so always be ready to pivot.

Be well-informed about the platform(s) you're on. Each has its own rules and strategies for catching the wave of the algorithm. Each has their own rules to avoid getting banned or restricted.

Your Online Image:

Judged Before You're Heard

Be aware of your online image. When people look you up, they are judging you. They judge your looks, your cars, your home, your clothes, even your hair! They judge your office, your location, your restaurant design.

People are professional judgers.

So, put the odds in your favor.

Become who you want to attract. If you want to attract a certain market or clientele, make sure that you have social media posts based around that.

If you are a fan of cars, make some posts about cars. If you are big on sports, make some posts about sports. If you want your posts to create attention, give your viewers something to talk about.

Remember, people like people that are like themselves. When someone goes to any of your social media, they want to see what things in common you have with them.

The Clean Image Checklist

Always have a clean image that represents your industry, your company, and your mission. There's a lot of people that have great products and services, but their social media does not represent that.

It's not enough to be posting consistently, you must post consistently and cleanly. Every post you make should be a strong representation of your brand/image. You want a clean image online, a clean website, with clean social media, so that when someone does find you or they do look you up, they can see themselves in business with you already.

Have a clean image ready to go.

Humanize Yourself

Those that know me know that I am very family oriented. Some of my best memories have been family experiences. I was fortunate enough to capture some of these on video.

One fun project that I did was with my grandma Harriet. My grandma loved her coffee. Because she was born in 1925, I thought it would be a fun idea to interview her about her life and experiences while we shared our morning coffee together. We had so much fun doing that, and those memories will last forever. I shared these experiences on social media. We named these interviews, *Coffee Talk with Grandma Harriet*.

I didn't realize that by showing this side of me, I was also humanizing myself for my audience. It made me more relatable.

I also shot a video showing me paying off my parents' debt. It was very heartfelt and impactful. I received numerous comments on the video from people I didn't even know, reaching out and saying that they could relate and had similar goals. Some of those people became clients and referral partners.

Don't be afraid to be vulnerable. You're not a machine; you're a human being. When you tell your story and share who you really are, like-minded people will find you.

You can still watch these videos on YouTube by the way!

What to Post

(Pain Points, Benefits, Proof)

Post videos, images, stories, company fliers, and industry related materials. Remember, people buy BENEFITS. They buy what your product or service DOES, not what it IS. Gather prospects by sharing statistics and stories of the *benefits* of your product or service.

Examples By Industry

If you're in the real estate industry, copy and paste updates relevant to the industry. Post interest rates for markets that are warm, hot, or cold. Give people information. Post content like, "5 Secrets to Lowering your Mortgage". Or "5 Secrets to Buying a Home, with Bad Credit".

6. Social Media

Make your posts relevant to the target market you are going after.

If you're in solar, talk about how people are saving money on their monthly utilities. Post updates regarding the rules and regulations that will BENEFIT the consumers.

If you're in life insurance, talk about how a family had financial security when someone passed away and there was no financial burden left on the family. You can post articles written about the tax-free cash value benefits of life insurance policies, or the long-term care benefits people can receive.

Share some of the stats such as: "Did you know that 72% of people in the US will need some form of Long-Term Care and 64% of bankruptcies are caused from medical bills?"

This stat alone most likely got you thinking about updating your life insurance. So, think about what a quality post would do for your viewers.

If you're in network marketing, let's say you're dealing in weight loss, talk about a customer testimonial of how someone lost weight using the product.

Whatever industry you're in, give relevant industry examples.

Search and Connect Strategy

I call this strategy search and connect. All this means is, you seek out the right people at the right time and in the right way.

Let's say you are a recruiter for your network marketing company. Well, that means you're going to be seeking salespeople. Same thing for insurance or roofing. How do you find them? Find who these people would be following on social media, and you'll find the people you're seeking. Here's how this strategy works step by step.

Step 1) What current gurus online would these people be likely to follow? Go to that guru's social media page.

Step 2) Look at the comments left on that guru's latest posts. Look for a comment that piques your interest.

Step 3) Personally message that person. Don't spam them! Just personally message those people.

An example opener for this could be:

"Hi, [potential prospect], I see we both follow [online guru]. What led you to start following them?"

The purpose of this is to find common ground. Psychology says that people like people that are like themselves. So, the fact that you were both following the same guru already puts something in common for you to talk about.

How This Worked for ME (Case Study)

When I was building my insurance business, I would use this strategy all the time. I followed different online influencers that specialized in different industries and topics.

Around 2015, PBD started gaining a lot of success with his Valuetainment channel. He would also do live events on Sunday nights where you could ask him questions. Patrick would post on his channel and people would leave comments. As I saw people posting, I would wait until I saw people post something positive that made sense to me. Then, I would reach out and say something like:

"Hi, I see we both follow Patrick Bet-David. I have been working directly with Patrick for the past several years. How has Patrick's advice helped your business?"

I did this over and over again for months at a time and ANYTIME I needed a boost in production. It led to further conversations and got me new clients and even new agents.

And the best part is: It's FREE!

Daily Posting Rhythm:

Stay on their Mind

On social media, your followers are seeing what you post and how often you are posting. They are testing you to see how consistent you will be. You're not going to get any traction by posting one video a month. With all the competition in the marketplace, that's not going to cut it. So, how often should you post?

One, it depends on your industry, but you want to post at least one to two times daily, whether that's free or sponsored content.

Two, you want to add value in everything you're posting. The goal is not to sell your product, but to add value and inform. There're too many videos and ads that are just pushing products. It's annoying!

Keep this in mind, *people hate to be sold but they love to buy*. They want the illusion of control that they made the decision. They want to feel empowered.

So, to summarize, the two things that you need to know right away are:

- Post consistently
- Add value

Use programs to post on all of your social media platforms simultaneously. Such as Hootsuite, Buffer, and Sprout Social.

Leverage AI (With Caution)

New tools like AI are changing the social media prospecting game in ways we can't imagine yet. By the time you read this book, technology has already been updated. So, any advice I can give you may already be outdated.

6. Social Media

When it comes down to setting up an AI program, there are different marketing companies that you can invest in to help with this. They use different types of bots and protocols to contact people that are in search of your products and service. However, that still does not help you work on your personal skill set.

AI can't improve your personal identity or your self-worth. Don't use AI as an excuse to not be prospecting. However, it's a fantastic tool for someone starting from zero. A prospector always needs to have the right resources and latest technology to stay ahead of the curve and leverage the latest marketing strategies. AI can help you do that while also helping you to comply with the TOS (terms of service) of social media marketing, which are also always changing.

There are also free programs that you can get that can link your social media channels together. This means that I can send out multiple videos at the same time daily on all my social media channels. You can set a time and date to automate when these videos are sent out. Keep in mind, like with any free program, you're getting what you pay for.

Personally, I've used a high-level CRM system that can also help with marketing and AI integration. There are companies you can hire to design specific AI marketing prospecting strategies perfect for your company. However, this could be costly and not everybody has the funds or resources to do so.

That's why you have this book. This book guides you to develop your personal skill set because only you have control of who you prospect, how you prospect, and why you prospect. Saying hello doesn't cost you anything. The first handshake doesn't cost anything. What you say after that is all skill, and that's all on you.

This advice should work in general: Always leverage the best tools that work for you.

AIM Wisely

Whatever program you buy, always know what your specific target market is. Know your **AIM**.

- **Age**

  Some products have age restrictions and requirements. Some products also serve a specific age group.

  For example, if you're in real estate, you may consider targeting married couples over 25 years of age. If you're trying to sell a 21-year-old a new home, they may not have the credit history or income to qualify.

  On the recruiting side, if you are in Network Marketing, you have to be 18 in the United States to start your business.

  The same with insurance. You have to be 18 in the United States to earn your license.

- **Income**

  You have a choice of what market you want to get into. Choose a market that can afford your product or service.

- **Market**

  Your product or service is going to fulfill a need. Whether you're serving lawyers, doctors or 9-5 blue collar workers, target the market that has the most need for your product or service. The old school saying is: ***The niche gets you rich***.

  Choose your AIM wisely, because whatever you *aim* at, you will hit.

FTC Rules & Income Claims:

Keep it Classy

Whatever you're selling on social media, whether it's a product, a service, or a recruitment, you have to be very careful to follow the FTC guidelines for enticing too much. Be very careful with false income claims, overexaggerating what your product or service can really do. This will bring you more problems than gain in the long term. However, you do want to sell your successful lifestyle. When people are checking out your social media, they're asking:

"Why would I wanna work with you?"

"What values are you bringing to me?"

"If I own that product, will I receive the same benefits?"

"Is that a quality product that will last?"

What Not to Do

There are many things I don't like seeing people do on social media. Avoid doing these things at all costs:

1. Don't mislead.

2. Don't be aggressive. Understand that not everyone you meet is open to buying right now.

3. Don't post any false claims. This is a big one! A lot of people in sales get into legal challenges by posting false claims or things that are not realistic.

4. Don't get banned! As I said before, each platform has its own rules. So, always follow your platform's guidelines.

Action Steps

Social Media Workflow

Here's a breakdown of the best practices, tailored to generate interest, build trust, and convert prospects into clients:

1. Identify Your Ideal Client

- Define your target audience: industry, job title, location, pain points.

6. Social Media

- Understand which platform they use most (LinkedIn for B2B, Instagram/TikTok for creative or lifestyle businesses, Facebook for local communities, etc.).

2. Choose the Right Platform(s)

- LinkedIn: Best for B2B, professionals, decision-makers.

- Instagram: Great for visual branding, lifestyle, products, and influencers.

- Facebook: Strong for community engagement and local businesses.

- Twitter/X: Good for thought leadership and real-time trends.

- TikTok/YouTube: If your product/service fits short or long-form video content.

3. Position Yourself as an Expert

Content = your calling card.

- Share educational, insightful, or entertaining content.

- Use a mix of:

  o Case studies

  o Tips & tricks

  o Industry news commentary

  o Behind-the-scenes

  o Testimonials

  o Engage with comments, messages, and shares promptly.

4. Engage Before Selling

Social selling = relationship building.

- Comment on their posts with value.

- React to their stories or content.

- Ask questions and DM with interest, not a pitch.

- Be genuinely curious and helpful first.

5. Use Direct Messaging Smartly

Cold DMs can work if done right:

- Personalize every message.

- Use Search & Connect strategy

6. Track and Optimize

Use tools like LinkedIn Sales Navigator, HubSpot, or Meta Business Suite to:

- Track engagement

- Follow up

- Measure effectiveness

- Refine your message based on what resonates.

Avoid:

- Mass-copy-paste DMs

- Pitching too early

- Ignoring comments or DMs

- Posting without interacting

Bonus Tools:

- CRM integration (e.g., with HighLevel or Salesforce)

- Social listening tools (Hootsuite, Sprout Social)

Next, turn to page 214 and fill in the charts I've given you there!

Chapter 7

Cold Market

Don't Break the Ice, Warm it Up

In 2018, I moved to Orlando, FL. Having grown up in South Florida, and having no warm market in Orlando, I was literally starting from scratch. I had to find a way to **become the unspoken mayor of the city**. Meaning, I had to go meet as many people as possible and make sure they knew who I was as well.

The first thing I did was to make a list of everywhere I could go to meet people:

Cigar lounge

Hookah lounge

7. Cold Market

The gym

The mall

A restaurant

A coffee spot

Networking event

Sporting event

Sport league

Private events

Private Masterminds

I then went online and found out where these places were meeting. I found out when different events were taking place and added them to my calendar. At that time, I made sure to **go to at least one networking event a day**. I worked tirelessly to build up my prospect list and network.

While attending these events, I noticed that not everybody knew how to properly network or have conversations.

It seems that we've all become socially awkward in the last several years! Making first contact with a stranger can be very challenging if you don't know what to say. What if there was a simple way to overcome your fear of making contact?

What if you could start random conversations anywhere you go and build genuine rapport quickly and confidently? If that sounds scary, here are *four simple steps* that you can take daily to overcome that fear. I call this *Approach and Connect*.

Approach and Connect

The challenge people face with Cold Prospecting is they have *approach anxiety*. They get in their head negative scenarios before they even happen. It's paralysis by analysis. Rather than taking action, they overthink.

The first mindset you can use to help you overcome approach anxiety is: Learn to be *interested* more than *interesting*. This will help shift your mindset from being worried about impressing people, to focusing on engaging with them. You can practice this new mindset by using Approach and Connect. It works in four easy steps.

Step 1) Compliment five people. You are not seeking anything from them, so there's no reason to be anxious. Simply notice what you like about them and then tell them that:

- I like your suit

- I love that jacket

It can even be as simple as opening the door for someone. Think about this, when was the last time someone gave you a genuine compliment? How did you feel when they did that? Didn't you want to continue to hear from this person?

Yes! The chances of continuing a conversation after you give a *genuine* compliment are higher than just *hoping* to start a conversation.

Do this EVERY day for three days. You will notice that people are genuinely nice.

Step 2) Notice someone's eye color while giving a compliment. The purpose of this is to help you "slow your roll" and look people in the eye with confidence. If you speak too fast, it can come across as low confidence.

- Compliment them

- Gently smile

- Notice their eye color

Do this for three days in a row no matter what.

Step 3) Step three is to follow the first two steps but then ask a question. You can say something like,

"Excuse me, I love that hat. Where did you get it?" or

"Excuse me, I love those shoes. Where did you get those?"

What you are going to notice with this is that most people are willing to have a conversation with you when you're genuinely interested in *them*.

Step 4) Repeat the previous three steps:

- Compliment five people

- Eye contact

- Ask a question.

As you're building up this repetition, you're going to start to see that people are not going to be rude; they're not going to be mean; they're going to be very open. This destroys your fear and builds up your confidence in yourself.

This opens the door to a genuine conversation, rather than just an interaction.

Conversation Starters

Here are a few ideas to help you start and continue conversations whether they are online, text, phone call, or in person.

Captain Obvious: Talk about what is currently happening. If there is a game on TV, talk about that. If there is good entertainment or good food at the event you are at, talk about that.

Make sense?

Season is the Reason (Cold Market): Talk about holidays, social media posts, birthdays, and sporting events that is relevant to your prospect. Engage them with what is engaging to them!

Are You in Real Estate or Mortgages? Asking this question is an easy conversation starter. Why? Because the majority of people that I see are usually in real estate or mortgages. Typically, people that are in real estate or mortgages dress classy and are professional.

If they say, "No, I'm not."

You can say, *"Oh, well you look like a realtor."*, and then continue the conversation.

If they say, "Yes, I am."

You can respond with a smile and say, "*I thought so.*", and then continue the conversation.

In reality, it doesn't matter whether they are or not, you just want to start a conversation.

Early in my career, I would sit at Starbucks right by the front door, where everybody walked in. I made sure that people would see me when they came in and when they went out. I even sat where people would wait for their drinks just so I had the opportunity to start a conversation. As people would walk by me, I would say with a confident and friendly tone:

"Real estate or mortgages?"

They'd stop in their tracks, smile, and respond:

"How did you know that?"

The funny part is, I was right most of the time. This has led to millions of dollars in commissions over the years.

The ABC's of Conversation

A genuine conversation can be broken down into three things: Opener, follow-up, and prospect. We can make this easier to remember by describing these three things as attention, befriend, and comfortable. That makes the acronym, ABC.

Attention) is as simple as making contact. This is your opener. An opener is giving attention to the person you want to meet. You've already learned how to do this in your four steps: Compliment, eye contact, question, follow-up. Be sure in your opener that you are:

- Smiling

- Speaking slowly

- Using a natural and level tone

Know what you want to say before you say it. Most people have *getting-ready to get-ready problems.* Don't fall into that trap. Be ready to make your opener before you make it, then make it.

Befriend) Once the opener is established, you need to maintain the conversation by having some kind of bridge into a deeper topic. This is something that connects you with the other person. Remember, people like people who are like themselves, so find common ground. Find something in common and talk about that. It has to be a genuine commonality. That's how you turn strangers into friends.

Comfortable) This is where you invite them to meet again. This is not where you sell them on something or offer to recruit them. They have to be comfortable with you before you can close with them.

You're simply inviting them to sit down to discuss your project or service. They have to be comfortable with you before they'll agree to meet with you, so work on establishing a common ground until they're comfortable with you. Then, you make your ask.

Don't be Shy: Networking Events

When I first started attending networking events, I did not get instant results. I was sometimes shy. I was not sure how to carry a conversation, and I was hoping people would just come up to me.

It never worked. An epiphany struck me when I went to three straight networking events but didn't make one connection. I realized that no one is at a networking event to be rude. Everyone is there for the same reason: To network!

Obvious, right?

People are there to make connections. You will never find a more open environment to approach a stranger. The only difference between a successful and unsuccessful networking event is your skill set to capitalize on the situation. Remember this:

Everything that we do is skill or will. You have the will to attend the event. Now it's up to you to work on your skill.

Don't Get Drunk: Networking Events

Don't fall back on liquid courage.

When you're at networking events, be careful not to drink too much. If you're of the legal drinking age, and you're a responsible adult, you're welcome to have a beverage. But if you have one too many, you're going to be perceived as irresponsible.

Rather than gaining the prospect, you're going to push them away.

Pay to Play

"Empty the coins from your purse into your mind and your mind will fill your purse with coins."
~Benjamin Franklin

When I first started in the insurance business, I flew across the country on my own dime to interview with a company I was not a part of. That is when I met

Patrick Bet-David. If I didn't invest in myself, putting my own time and money in to walk into that room, my life would be VERY different right now.

Investing in yourself will always have the greatest ROI. Investing in events will also put you in greater proximity to the people you need to meet. At these events, you will find people of a different caliber. Higher caliber people are typically found in rooms that are harder to get into. That can be a private business club, a private cigar lounge, or VIP seating at a convention.

I am a member of several private clubs, and I also make sure to find the most elite ticket available at events, because I only want to connect with serious like-minded individuals. When I first started in business, I did not have the funds to have all the memberships and VIP seating. I simply worked my way up!

1) Make a list of private clubs, networking events, and conventions that are in your area.

2) Find out their membership/attendance fees.

3) Decide if the network and the environment is worth your time.

It is much easier to work with like-minded people. Whether that is as a client, a recruit, or a referral source. There are a multitude of events and networking events that are held around the world. Most of these events are not free. Sometimes you must "Pay to Play".

If the event has a registration fee, consider what market you want to prospect in and where they will be sitting at that event.

If there are private rooms just for the VIP's, find a way to be in that room. Being with the people that paid to play as opposed to the ones that just show up, helps separate *you*, a pro, from the posers.

Work the Room: Networking Events

Actively work the room. People paid to be there to get something from the event. The majority of the time, they are also there for the same reason you are, which is to: **Connect with the right people**.

So go and be that right connection.

One of the best places to meet new people is at networking events. You can go online and search for:

[Your city]

[Type of the event]

[Who will be there]

When you go there, how do you stick out from everyone else? Most people do not know how to have a conversation at events. Most of the time, they make the mistake of making their conversations all about themselves. Over the years, I've learned a way to have a simple conversational flow while networking.

7. Cold Market

Learn **PROM**

Personal

Recreation

Occupation

Meet

Here's how this works:

Personal – Ask questions about their background. Where they grew up. Ask about their family, kids, what sports are the kids into, etc.

Recreation – Do they play or follow sports? Do they like to travel? Where have they traveled? Etc.

Occupation – What line of work are they in? How can you add value to their business?

Meet – Who at the networking event can you introduce them to? Find out who they want to meet.

Building Credibility by Edifying Others

I remember back in 2013, I went to a networking event at the Blue Martini in Miami. Several of my coworkers came with me. Everyone had a name tag. And each name tag had a color designated to an industry. Tech was blue. Finance was green. And so on. While I was working the room with my buddy, Kehinde, who at that time had been in finance close to 15 years, I bumped into a girl named Brittany. Brittany at that time was working for a financial company and mentioned that she is looking at switching firms or starting her own.

I asked Kehinde to join us in the conversation. First, I *EDIFIED* Kehinde and his background. I made it sound as if Kehinde is a genius in the financial world (he actually is, so that made it easy). Brittany's perception of Kehinde gave him power-position and leverage. For a full two minutes, I bragged about Kehinde to her in front of him. THEN, I excused myself to get a drink (I prefer water to stay sharp) and left Kehinde and Brittany talking. You know what Kehinde did the entire time I was away?

He was re-edifying ME and giving me the power position.

What that showed is a culture of trust between coworkers, which is an environment that prospects want to be around. Too many companies have a cut-throat mindset that ends up pushing people out the door.

Learn to leverage a trusted coworker when you are new, and that will give you a competitive advantage and build your credibility.

Step 1) Edify your coworker.

Step 2) Walk away just long enough to give your coworker time to edify you back.

Choosing the Right Events

I went to a real estate networking event once — 99% of the people at this event were realtors. I was in insurance, so 99% of the people around me were prospects. But for them, 99% of the room were *competitors*. They were talking to people which they would never send business to or receive business from. That's not a networking event.

That's a bar hangout.

Here's the thing, it's okay to go to a convention of your peers *if* you are there for your own education. But that is *NOT* a networking event. Don't mistake educational events for networking events.

You want to be in rooms where your prospects are, not where your competitors are.

Sit with a Purpose

To initiate the ABC's of a conversation with a stranger, you first need to be in the right place for conversations to be initiated. So, sit with a purpose.

When you're going out to eat, sit where it's easy to start a conversation, either at a table in the middle of the restaurant or at the bar. Sit in the middle of the bar so that there's people to the left and right of you. If you're sitting in the back corner like Tony Soprano, you're not going to meet people.

Other Things Not to Do

When you're prospecting your cold market, there are a few things to avoid.

First, don't speak like every other person.

For example, if you compliment someone by saying, *"You look sharp!"* you sound like every other network marketing or insurance agent out there.

Think of something unique and genuine to say instead. Don't give a compliment and immediately go in for the kill. If you give me a compliment such as, "You look sharp!" and then the next thing out of your mouth is to invite me to your office, I can see straight through that. I know that you're not being sincere and that you're an amateur.

Don't smirk. Smirking can be taken as sarcasm. Smile genuinely and with teeth.

Don't be overzealous. People can tell if your energy is fake. If you're fake, I know that you're trying to convince me of something.

The top prospectors are professional sorters, not convincers.

Hygiene

Make sure your hair, nails, and clothes are good. You want to look polished, not slick. Do not smoke cigarettes or other similar products when you are prospecting. Not many of the top performers smoke, but even if you do, that smell gets on your clothes. It causes bad breath and turns prospects away.

Showing that you can take care of your hygiene shows the prospect that you can take care of them.

Prospecting the Opposite Sex

The challenge in prospecting someone of the opposite sex of you is that people can think you're hitting on them. That shuts the door immediately. The solution to prospecting the opposite sex is:

1) Only talk business. Do not bring up flirtatious talk.

2) Leverage a *sideline* of the same sex of the person you are prospecting.

For example, if you are a girl prospecting a guy, you can say: "Hey Jon! What type of business are you in? I would love to introduce you to my coworker, Mike, he is an expert in [the business] and you two would have a lot in common."

The reverse is true if you are a guy prospecting a girl.

If you are married or are in a relationship, make sure you find a way to naturally mention this in the beginning of your conversation. This will disarm the prospect and confirm that your intentions are professional.

Sort, Don't Convince

Your job as a prospector is to sort through the people you want to do business with, not convince people to do business with you.

Convincing is coming from force. You never want to force people to do business with you. That's setting things up for failure. Sorting is simply knowing that there are people that need and value your product or service. You are looking for those that are looking for you; they just don't know it yet.

Your job is to sort through the people with questions such as,

"Would you like to make more money?"

"Would you like to have a guaranteed income when you retire?"

"Do you feel you are being paid what you're worth? If not, would you be open to a conversation?"

"Would you like a more fulfilling career?"

If I was prospecting you, and you answered yes to 80% of those questions, I can help you. If you didn't, you're not the right person, and I'm not going to convince you.

Sort the right people, don't waste your time trying to convince the wrong people.

Lunch and Learn

It's easier to catch more fish when you're throwing out a net vs. a fishing line.

Rather than prospecting one person at a time, if you could put a group of prospects together at the same time, it would help speed up results. Some people spend thousands of dollars on mailers to try and organize events with no guaranteed return on investment. The most cost-effective way is to introduce yourself to people of influence and ask to set up a Lunch & Learn.

Lunch & Learns and other similar types of speaking events are the same concept of **throwing out a net**.

For Lunch & Learns, you want to speak with business owners or people of influence that can rally a group of people together and allow you to present your product or service.

Not having a strong warm market when I first moved to Orlando, I met the VP of marketing for a beverage company at a local cigar lounge. After building a relationship, we discussed having me speak to a group of his friends. He was able to put together a group of ten of his friends for lunch. While they enjoyed their lunch, I educated them on the benefits of insurance products.

That one sit-down led to a few thousand dollars short of a six-figure commission. All it cost me was the price of a few hoagies.

You provide the food. They provide the people!

Buying Leads

This comes down to your industry. I've been in the insurance business for sixteen years, and I don't buy leads. However, there are some insurance platforms that solely rely on purchased leads. The challenge with ONLY relying on bought leads is:

1) They are expensive and the cost continues to rise.

2) Laws continue to change on who you can and cannot call.

3) Most leads are not fresh.

4) If you need to make more sales, it's not as easy as *just buy more leads*. The reason I say that is because if you're already working ten hours a day, you don't have much more time to give.

5) Most people in sales don't have the money to continuously come out of pocket to pay for leads.

I have personally seen sales organizations make millions of dollars utilizing quality lead programs. Yes, they do exist. If that's the route you want to go, make sure that you have the proper budget and continuous lead generation programs up to date.

The purpose of this book is, if you don't have the money to buy leads, how can you still generate business? If you do have the money to buy leads, don't leave money on the table by not maximizing other lead generation resources.

Overcoming Resistant Markets:

The Shoe Story

I remember a story Patrick Bet-David told me years ago. When he was in the financial industry, he wanted to work with specific doctors. The challenge with trying to get in front of doctors is that they have gatekeepers who we know as *secretaries*. So Patrick went out and bought multiple pairs of new shoes. He also bought boxes to put one shoe in. He would then make a list of all the doctors he wanted to meet, get their address, and mail them a box with one shoe in it. When the secretary would get the mail and open the box, there will also be a letter in the box.

The letter would read: "Hi, Doctor [So and So], my name is Patrick Bet-David. I'm a financial professional in the area. And I would love the opportunity to work with you. The reason there is a shoe in the box is to let you know **I already have one foot in the door.** I would love the opportunity to get the other foot in. I hope you can appreciate my sense of humor, and I look forward to meeting with you soon."

I'm sure that you smiled or laughed when you read this. Well get this, the secretary probably laughed too. Because that was a humorous and original idea, the secretary, more often than not, would go and show the doctor the letter.

Finding creative and fun ways to start conversations makes the prospecting process exciting and more effective.

Here's another example.

Lightbulb. Send a packaged lightbulb and say, "I have a *bright* idea for you!"

Seeds. Send a box of seeds and say, "I've already planted the seed. I'd love the opportunity to grow our business relationship!"

The Secret Sauce to Cold Prospecting

The secret sauce to cold prospecting is very simple: **Don't focus on the outcome, focus on the connection**. People can tell quickly when you have an agenda or ulterior motive. If your motive is to make a genuine connection, you will always have a positive outcome.

Also, you cannot control the outcome. You can only control your number of attempts to make new connections.

Action Steps

Your action steps to take away from this chapter is to practice. Practice the five steps I taught you to build up your confidence. When you're ready, practice the ABC's of conversation. This week:

- Talk to everybody.

  - Use the three-foot rule: Anyone that's within three feet of you, talk to them.

- Compliment five strangers, noticing their eye color and using a follow-up question.

- Have an ABC conversation with three strangers.

- Use **APA**

  - **Approach**

    Compliment or Question

  - **Prospect**

    Ask a question relevant to the outcome you are looking for.

    Examples

    Recruiting: Do you keep your options option?

    Sales: Would you be open to?

    Sales: Have you considered?

  - **Ask**

    Set up a follow-up time

PART III

Chapter 8

Mastering the Follow-Up

Fortune is in the follow-up.

That's a phrase that comes from a simple understanding: Following up with people shows that you're serious about what you do; shows that you believe in what you're selling; shows that you're not going anywhere; and shows that your prospect can trust you.

People rarely give you a yes on the first contact. They need time to process what you spoke about. So, if you don't follow up, the entire conversation can go to waste. Think about it like this, if I went out and bought leads, but I never followed up with those leads, I just threw away my money and wasted my time. I could try and justify myself and say, 'The leads are not good!'

In reality, I didn't put in the work.

Don't be discouraged by how many times it takes to follow-up to close a deal. It typically takes 5 follow-up attempts after the initial contact to close 80% of sales.[1]

A way to stay positive through this process is to **look at each of your follow up conversations as a countdown to a 'Yes.'** Look forward to your next follow up, because each one is getting you closer to your sale.

---

[1] MTD Sales Training, "Sales Follow Up Statistics You Need to Know," MTD Sales Training Blog, July 22, 2020, https://www.mtdsalestraining.com/mtdblog/sales-follow-up-statistics.html.

Set Up Your Next Follow-up

During your First

At the end of each of your follow-up conversations, get something on the books for your next follow-up. You want to be able to get in front of your prospect again as soon as possible. Think about it like this: When bread comes out of the oven, it's nice and hot and soft, and it tastes delicious. If you let that bread sit out for too long, it gets cold and hardened and more difficult to eat.

The sooner you follow up, the warmer that contact still is, and the more likely they are to close. Setting up your next follow-up before ending your current conversation allows you to maintain this momentum and keep the bread warm.

8. Mastering the Follow-up

Organize your Follow-ups

Write things down so you don't forget. You can choose different options, such as:

CRM Systems

Spreadsheets

Cell phone calendar

Old school paper calendar

Choose what fits you and your organization the best. **Caution**: Don't call the same prospect every single day. It shows desperation and that you have nothing else going on.

A simple solution would be to:

- Try following up 2 days in a row

- If you don't make contact, skip for 2 days in a row

- Follow up again, but hold off if it falls on a weekend

- Then try once a week

- Then try once a month

The idea here is to stay determined, but also to pace yourself so you're not getting overwhelmed or worse, overwhelming your prospect.

Follow Up Using

Season is the Reason

There is always a reason to follow up. Use the current events or season to follow up with someone. That can be a holiday, something in the media, or someone's post online.

Use any excuse you genuinely can: Birthdays, special events, funny stories, etc. When you notice something going on that you already have in common with the prospect, reach out about it.

For example, if they're racing fans: "Did you watch the F1 race today?"

8. Mastering the Follow-up

If they're basketball fans: "Did you watch the NBA Finals today"

If they're into tennis: "Did you see Wimbledon on TV today?"

The secret sauce to following up is to continue a conversation. If you had a conversation with a prospect and it went well, write down what you talked about. Then, it could be weeks or even months later, when you notice that topic comes up (however it does), continue that conversation with that prospect based on your new information.

For example, if I meet someone on the basketball court, I can follow up with that person months later when the NBA Finals are starting. Continue the conversation by basing it on a current event that's relevant and related to your older conversation. It's that easy.

The best script in the world is common sense. Here are some commonsense scripts you can model for your follow-up conversations.

8. Mastering the Follow-up

Common Sense

Follow-Up Scripts

Start your follow-up by continuing the conversation:

"Oh, hey Jacob! Any plans for the holiday this weekend? I remembered how you said you might be planning on taking your family up to the lake house..."

Next, just let the conversation flow naturally. There's no script for this. Just genuinely talk.

Next, transition the conversation back to your pitch:

"Listen, Jacob, I hope you enjoyed your weekend. I'm sorry that I've been busy lately and haven't had a chance to reach back out to you regarding [solar, insurance, etc.]. I know setting up your [solar, insurance, etc.] was important to you, and I wanted to see you when I can squeeze you into our schedule this coming week."

Lastly, confirm a time they can talk. If you can't confirm a time, rinse and repeat the process of continuing the conversation until you can reach a proper follow-up.

Don't Follow-up Like Everyone Else

I've said this many times now, the part you play in prospecting is not to sound like everyone else. There's got to be a high-level of take-away and value you're giving to your prospect on every meeting you make with them. There's a key to the script I just gave you that you might not have picked up on...

Notice how I did not say the typical, 'Hey, I wanted to circle back...' or 'You haven't gotten back to me yet...' People hear this all the time. Hold yourself to a higher standard.

Instead of saying, 'You haven't gotten back to me on my offer' say 'I haven't gotten back to you.' This reframes the conversation, putting the responsibility on yourself for not (yet) providing the value you're confident in to your prospect. This is the psychology of follow-up.

You can take this a step even further. Take a look at this example script:

"I'm sorry to get back to you so late. My schedule has been back-to-back lately. I know the last time we spoke this [solar, life insurance, etc.] was important to you, shall I take you off my follow-up list? Or would you like to set up a time to take care of the situation? The ball's in your court!"

Don't be afraid to put the pressure on. **You can't be afraid to lose a prospect you never had in the first place**. This is how you sort through to the people you want to work with.

Take it Away

We spoke in our last chapter how we don't want to convince people on our offer. Rather, we want to *sort through* to the people who are already open, they just don't know about your offer yet.

Putting pressure on the prospect is your surest way to know whether they are the right person for you. If they know they're not going to hear from you again, they may be more enticed to reach out and close the deal. People like getting a good deal, but they *hate* losing one.

Don't drive yourself nuts trying to convince people. It's like only trying to convince a romantic interest to like you when they just don't. Don't force it. If a prospect is not motivated about your offer, it's a waste of your time, time that you should be using finding someone motivated.

Don't Rely on the One

I'll speak about this last point further. Having plenty of options means you can go into any follow-up with the confidence in knowing that, if they don't like your offer, there's someone else who will. This is called having a pipeline.

You want to have confidence in your ability to connect with people. You need to *know* that there's a lot of people out there looking for your product and service, you just need to get better at your skill. If you're relying on one big sale or one prospect to change your game, then you have the wrong mindset. It tells me that you're an amateur in business and you're trying to get lucky.

Amateur prospectors try to get lucky based on their personality, wit, or their good looks.

Professional prospectors get consistent leads based on skill set and value.

Follow-up Things Not to Do

Don't call every day, day after day. Nobody likes a pest.

Don't get frustrated.

Don't be afraid of rejection or the person not getting back to you.

Don't be pushy.

Don't sound like everybody else.

A Follow-up Story

This story I'm about to share taught me it's never too late to follow-up and it's okay (and often preferrable) to show that you're willing to walk away.

I met someone on social media. Let's say his name was Joel. He had a 7-figure bank account and wasn't sure of the best way to manage his finances. We spoke as many as six times and still had not closed the deal. Then, he dodged three of my calls over the course of a month. Finally, I decided to send him this text message:

"Hey, I know we've both been busy and keep missing each other, but I also don't want to keep following up if you're not serious. I know the last

time that we spoke, you wanted to protect your money and get guaranteed income. Is that something you still want to do for yourself? I'm more than happy to help. I'll leave the ball in your court."

Within 30 minutes, I got a phone call. He became a client right then and there. The client has to know that you're willing to walk away. The prospect has to know that you have other options. It's just like in dating: The pretty people have multiple options, and they seek people who have multiple options.

It's Never too Late to Follow-up

If you've let a lead go, it's never too late to follow up with them again. In fact, you can use it to your advantage by working that into the script:

"Hey, Justin. It's been a long time. The tennis match was on (or whatever your conversation topic might be), and it made me think of you. How are things?"

Then you have the conversation, transition to your follow-up, and confirm. It doesn't matter how long it's been or if you've dropped the ball: find an excuse to reach out.

Sometimes it's even essential to wait a long time to follow-up again. If you get a 'Not now' response, you can say something like:

"Not a problem. I understand life happens. Are you okay if I follow up in 90 days?"

If they completely say no, then sort through that person.

Action Points

Follow-ups are the same technique no matter what industry you're in. Here's some action steps you can do this week to improve your follow-up game:

1. Make a list of everybody that you've met in the last 30 days, 90 days, six months, and one year.

8. Mastering the Follow-up

2. Write down what you talked about the last time you spoke with each person. Develop what your opener can be (sports, politics, interests, holidays, etc.)

3. Practice follow-ups with each person on your list.

If you need an example sheet of what this could look like, turn to pg. 216 of this book! You can even write in it yourself.

Chapter 9

Prospecting Habits and Behaviors

I say it again, understand the difference between things you can and cannot control. You cannot control the outcome of a prospect's response. You can control:

- What you say – your words

- Who you say it to –your market

- How many times you say it – your work ethic

Everything that we do is a skill.

Prospecting is a skill, not a talent. It's not about having natural charisma or good looks. Rather, it's a skill you have to practice *daily* to get good. Remember this: **success is not what you do, it's what you do *daily*.**

What Separates Pros from Amateurs

There are two main differences between a top prospector's daily routine versus an amateur's. **First**, an amateur does not have a daily routine dedicated to prospecting. This is their daily mistake. You can't wing it. You can't just say, "Hey I'll prospect whenever I can."

No, you have to dedicate time for prospecting. Prospecting is a discipline.

A professional prospector has daily time dedicated to prospecting each of their four markets: warm, referrals, social media, and cold. Whether you work all four of those each day, or focus on just one per day, make it a part of your daily routine.

Whatever business you're in, if you are new, prospecting engaged leads and getting them into your pipeline should be 80% of your day. Anything less, and you're getting busy to get busy.

Second, an amateur thinks that prospecting is only for some days of the week. Wrong. Prospecting needs to be on your mind all the time. This is a skill set but also a mindset. Think about it like this: Everywhere you go is the possibility of a prospect. Everyone you meet is either a candidate for your offer or knows a candidate for your offer. Everything is an opportunity.

It's an amateur that says, "I'm not in my prospecting mood, so I'm not gonna prospect this person."

A professional says, "Prospecting is my daily skill set and mindset. I'm going to practice and therefore strengthen that every day."

If you're in business, you're in the prospecting business. It's not just a tool you do when you feel like it. Especially if you're in sales, prospecting is your profession. If you are new, or you are trying to reignite your business, **80% of your day should be prospecting**. Most people quit business in the first year or two because they haven't done that work on the front end. Their leads dry up and the business dies.

DMA's: Daily Checklist

DMA stands for Daily Monitoring Activities. A successful day should be constructed with the same repetitive actions that will produce a clear result, which is to *increase your prospect list*.

Depending on your industry, you should be hitting a certain number of new prospects per day. I have found that meeting five new prospects a day is a healthy number to aim for without overwhelming yourself. There are several steps you can take to ensure you hit this target.

First, find out who your ideal client is and where they hang out. Let's say I'm looking for people that are over 25 years old, married, have children, and that take their money seriously. Where do those people hang out in the morning before work? It might be at a popular coffee spot, or maybe they gather at a business club for lunch. That means I need to be there too, networking.

If you're struggling to think of places, use the list I used when I first came to Orlando, on pg. 135.

The point is you should be able to prospect anywhere and everywhere you go. Make prospecting part of your daily routine.

This works for any of your four markets and could take place anywhere. For example, if you're working your social media market on a certain day, then the place you 'go' will be forums or pages where your target market congregates.

Second, find as many networking events based around your industry as possible. Go make connections. It's that simple.

Third, follow-up. Work the contact information of everyone you meet every day into your CRM and follow up with each one of them. It doesn't matter what market you're working, one of the keys to being successful is setting aside a specific time to prospect and *then to follow up with* prospects.

Four, have a dedicated schedule for all of these things. I have a daily schedule for when I'm meeting new people, attending a networking event, and am following up.

Schedule for these three simple things that you should be doing every day:

- Meeting new people

- Networking

- Following up

You're doing these three things every day in terms of your core four:

- Warm market

- Referrals

- Social media

- Cold market

It is also good to have time for self-education on your daily schedule. However, while personal development is important, be careful that it doesn't become prospect avoidance. A lot of people use the excuse, *I need to know more first*, that they become so busy *getting-ready to get-ready*, they end up wasting time and never achieve their desired results.

Don't use personal development as an excuse for inaction.

What if I Don't Have the *Time* to Prospect?

If you're part-time in business or you have a part-time job that gives you limited time, that doesn't mean you don't have time to prospect. Rather, it just means you need to be more specific in your schedule and more diligent in your discipline.

There's nothing stopping you from getting up 30 minutes earlier, going into a coffee spot that has a high influx of people, and giving yourself a chance to meet one person. There's nothing stopping you from taking 15 minutes on your lunch break to send out 15 messages on social media. There's nothing stopping you from making 3 follow-up calls on your lunch break.

You cannot control time, but you can control YOUR time.

You cannot control who picks up the phone, but you can control how many dials you make...

You cannot control how many people respond to your messages or videos, but you can control how many messages and videos you sent out...

You cannot control others...

You can control yourself, your time, your behaviors, and your discipline.

Build Confidence by Keeping
Promises to Yourself

It's not enough to have a good daily schedule. You have to follow through on it. Keeping your commitment to your daily routine builds your confidence. Keep your promises to yourself.

Most people don't have confidence because they don't trust themselves. They don't keep their word to themselves. Well, how are other people gonna trust you if you can't trust yourself? Remember, the fortune is in the follow-up, but it's also in the follow-through. Build your confidence as a prospector by keeping your daily promises.

There's No Such Thing as Burnout

I've heard this phrase so many times that it's funny to me!

9. Building Daily Habits

Burnout means you don't enjoy what you're doing. If you're using that term to describe your daily routine, it means you're not focused on a clear goal. It's an excuse. When I hear people say, "I'm so burned out!" I say, "You're not burned out! You're bored!"

Think about it like this. Would you be *burned out* if you were making $1,000,000 a month, having fun with your work, helping other people, and traveling the world? Probably not. You're *burned out* because you don't enjoy what you're doing.

It's that simple.

If you're not *excited* when you wake up in the morning about your work, you're either doing the wrong work or you're working wrong. Then, you have to ask yourself why you're not excited about it. Are you not making the money that you desire? Are you not getting the result that you desire? I promise you this, if you're making a lot of money and getting a lot of results, if you're having fun at your *job*, you're never going to be burned out.

9. Building Daily Habits

This advice can apply to you even if you're already in your dream job. Sometimes people dive into the busy work of their dream business to avoid prospecting. Then they get *burned out*. They wonder why they've lost their passion for what they love to do.

What they don't realize is, they're acting from fear. They get everything ready just to get ready.

They tell themselves that they're working harder than they really are. But they're not actually doing the real work, the most important aspect of business, which is getting more business. **So, it feels like you're working hard, but you're actually just making work hard.** There's a big difference of mindset between those two things.

If you're feeling burnt out, either you're in the wrong job or you're doing the right job in the wrong way. If that's you, this next section will teach you how to get excited about your life and work again.

Getting Over Your "Burnout"

The key to getting out of burnout is to find a worthy goal. Find something you want to go after. Find something that you want to be in the hunt for. This can be a short-term goal. Even a goal just for today. Set it, then go after it. Make sure that it gives the results that you want. Then, it won't feel like *work* when you're working towards it.

Action Steps

1. **Time-Block your Prospecting Hours**

   o Choose specific times each day dedicated to warm, referral, social media, and cold market prospecting.

   o Treat these hours like non-negotiable appointments.

2. Pick your Prospecting Arena

- Ask: *Where do my people hang out today?*

  - In person? Go there.

  - Online? Get in those DMs.

  - Event? Show up sharp and ready.

3. Meet 5 New People Today

- Doesn't matter the market, start five conversations.

- Document their info, drop them into your CRM, and label the type of lead.

4. Follow Up with 3 People Daily

- Use voice notes, personal texts, or a check-in message that adds value (not a pitch).

- Keep a log: Who did you follow up with, and how did they respond?

5. **Schedule One Networking Event Per Week (at least)**

   ○ Choose based on where your ideal client or strategic partners show up.

   ○ Bonus: Attend with a goal: *meet three new contacts* and *follow up within 24 hours.*

6. **Make a 3-Promise Checklist Every Morning**

   ○ Write down three things you promise yourself you'll do that day for your business.

   ○ Hit all three = confidence compound.

7. **Log 10 Minutes of Personal Development**

   ○ Read a page. Watch a clip. But only if you're taking action from it.

○ Ask: *What will I apply today from what I just learned?*

8. **Reframe Burnout as Misalignment**

○ If you feel drained, don't retreat, *redirect.*

○ Ask yourself: *What result am I chasing today?* Then go hunt it.

9. **Create a Visual Goal Trigger**

○ Print a picture of your target: a home, a dollar amount, a lifestyle, a client you want to serve.

○ Look at it every morning before you start prospecting.

10. **Track Your Wins and Lessons**

• End each day with two entries:

○ One *win* from the day (even if small).

○ One *lesson* you'll improve tomorrow.

Chapter 10

Prospecting Scenarios: What to Do & When

This chapter uses a rapid-fire Q&A format to tackle common prospecting situations. The goal is to equip you with real-world tactics and mindsets you can apply immediately.

Q. What do you do when a prospect ghosts you?

A. Let's say you make a really good connection with someone. They're an engaged lead and you're about to move in on closing. Suddenly, they ghost you! What do you say?

First, don't chase. You have to have the confidence to take away your offer. Secondly, gently confirm your upcoming conversation or sit down.

10. Prospecting Scenarios

This adds a little gentle obligation that, if the person hears this message, they will tend to keep their appointment. However, be prepared to cancel the appointment and replace it with another. Lastly, put the ball back in their court with a **sort, don't convince** statement. Here's how this works in the form of a script:

"Jon, I enjoyed our convo the other day. I'm looking forward to continuing it at 3pm tomorrow."

If they continue to ghost you, send a message like this a few days later:

"My apologies for not getting back to you. I've been nonstop this week. Last time we spoke, you wanted to look at [the offer]. I'm more than happy to squeeze you in if you're serious, but I'll leave it up to you. Let me know where you want to go from here."

That puts the ball in their court. Reiterate what they said; put the pressure back on them. Don't be afraid to walk away. Again, your attitude is *sort, don't convince*. In summary, your steps are:

- Apologize for not connecting.

- Reiterate the prospect's past interest.

- Use takeaway posture: "Let me know where you want to go from here."

Q. How do you handle trolls & negativity?

A. In business, having thick skin is part of the game. If you're afraid of being judged, you're gonna have a hard time in business. You have to build mental toughness.

Keep in mind:

"Mediocre people cannot stand high achievers. High achievers cannot stand mediocre people."

-Nick Saban

Let's say you make a social media post about your life insurance offer, and an agent from another company comments, "That's trash, that's a rip-off."

So what? Don't get sucked in. Let them be miserable.

10. Prospecting Scenarios

One of my favorite phrases is: "Dogs don't bark at parked cars."

If you're doing something worthwhile, someone's gonna hate. Let them. Don't delete. Don't argue. Just keep going. Haters are a sign you're doing something worth noticing.

Q. What if I'm awkward or nervous?

A. People are afraid of being awkward. Everyone is awkward at first. It's a process. The process goes like this:

Awkward → Mechanical → Natural

I remember one of my new sales reps was making calls to his warm market. The script he was reading was supposed to read like this:

"Hey, Jon, it's Jim! I just took a new position with a financial firm and I'm really excited about it. I need to do ten sit-downs in the next week to get

some experience under my belt or else I may miss out on my certification. Is there a way you'd be able to help me by being one of my sit-downs?"

Instead, the sales rep said:

"Hey, Jim, I'm excited!", and then he hung up the phone!

That had to rank in my top ten hardest laughs of all time! I was literally in tears laughing.

My point is that when you first start doing anything, it's *awkward*. You've never done it before. As you get better, you get *mechanical*. You're following a script. It sounds robotic. Eventually, you become *natural*. That's who you are. You're standing up with your shoulders back. You're smiling. You're you.

Every pro was once a rookie. The goal is to keep moving forward.

Q. What if I can't get referrals?

10. Prospecting Scenarios

A. If you ask a client for a referral and they say something like, "I don't feel comfortable vouching for anyone,"

Ask them, "*I can appreciate that. Is there something I can improve on where you would feel comfortable making a connection?*"

If they bought from you but won't refer you, they didn't have a good experience with you. That's on you. Good service leads to referrals. Bad service doesn't.

You have to own that. Referrals are earned, not owed. Here's the step-by-step:

Ask if they're satisfied.

If they are, ask who else you can help.

If they aren't satisfied, fix the problem.

Q. What If a Strategic Partner Says No?

A. Move on. Don't try to convince someone to work with you if they don't see the value.

10. Prospecting Scenarios

When it comes to strategic partnerships, you want just that, *partners*. If someone doesn't see the value in collaborating, that's not your person. Utilize your mindset of non-attached. Your steps are:

- Collaborate with the willing.

- Don't *sell* the value of your partnership, just *show* it.

- If they don't get it, next!

Bringing it all Together:

Take Massive Action

I want to leave you with certain key points and a mindset to keep in mind.

It doesn't matter which section of prospecting you're in: You have to take massive action. If you're working your warm market, you actually have to contact your warm market.

If you're looking for referrals, you have to ask for referrals and build specific relationships to get those referrals to come in consistently.

If it's social media, you actually have to post on social media things of value in a consistent manner.

If it's a cold market, you actually have to go to networking events to build relationships. You have to be able to go out and talk to people and start conversations.

It all starts with you taking massive action!

90 Day Lag Time

You are prospecting to build a pipeline. A pipeline is your lifeline. It takes time to build it. The work you are doing now will most likely show up in 90 days.

So, don't get frustrated if you don't get instant results. Stay consistent stuffing the pipeline. The faster you do that, the sooner the prospects will move forward with you.

For example, if you talk to someone on Monday at a coffee shop, it may take a month for that person to have a coffee with you to discuss business. That's normal and a part of the process.

Stay consistent with your follow-up.

Make Personal Development a Priority

Sales is the most rewarding and frustrating industry at the same time. This is why, on average, salespeople earn the highest income. Selling is not about being pushy or aggressive. Selling is simply asking questions and solving problems. The better you get at asking questions and solving bigger problems, the more money you're going to make.

The challenge is, too many sales professionals don't give themselves enough time to discover the secrets of their craft. They get frustrated and discouraged too easily. Personal development will help eliminate fear, doubt, and frustrations. *As you continue to work on your mindset, your skill set will grow.* Make reading, attending business events, watching training videos, or anything that will sharpen your mindset a priority.

Don't worry about being perfect. The key is to DO. Learn as you go and make little adjustments along the way. Find out what the person is unhappy with and communicate how you are the solution.

Success is not what you do, it's what you do daily!

This book is a foundation. If you want to dive in deeper and connect with me, I can be reached at:

I look forward to hearing from you.

I wish you all the best on your journey to mastering the SECRETS of PROSPECTING!

Appendix

This is the teaching tool of the book. Here you'll find interactive activities, script templates, and extra information on such topics as:

Door-to-Door prospecting

Mastering phone calls

Social Media Workflow

Prospecting to close

KYC Chart

Field	Client Entry
Full Name	
Client's Date of Birth	
Mailing Address	
Phone Number	
Email Address	
Spouse's Name	
Spouse's Date of Birth	
Children's Names & DOBs	
Favorite Food	
Favorite Restaurant	
Favorite Beverage/Wine	
Favorite Sports Team	
Anniversary Date	
Shoe Size	
Favorite Color	

Favorite Candy	
Favorite Snack	
Favorite Way to De-Stress	
Favorite Music/Band	
Favorite Movie	
Favorite Animal	
Notes	

Social Media Checklist

Item	Your Plan
What Industry Are You In?	
Industry News Source	
Value-driven Message	
Social Media Platforms	
Days per Week to Post	
Times per Day to Post?	
Post Scheduling App	
Target Audience — Age	
Target Audience — Income	
Target Market / Niche	
Performance Tracker	
Types of Content	
Weekly Goal for Engagement	

Posting Weekly Schedule

Day	Platform Used	# of Posts Made	Type of Content	Notes / Adjustments
Monday				
Tuesday				
Wednesday				
Thursday				
Friday				
Saturday				
Sunday				

#	First Name	Last Name	R/F/A*	Contact Profile #	Last Conversation	Next Opener	Follow-Up Date	Status / Result	Notes
1									
2									
3									
4									
5									
6									
7									
8									
9									
10									
11									
12									
13									
14									
15									

R/F/A* = Relative / Friend / Acquaintance

Profile (quick tags):

1. 25+ years
2. Married
3. Has Children
4. Homeowner
5. Earns Income
6. Ambitious
7. Dissatisfied
8. Business-Minded

A Prospecting Pro's Daily Schedule

■ **Green = APE Sh#t Time → Appointments, Phone Calls, Events**

These are the income-producing, in-the-business hours.

■ **Yellow = Administrative / Prep**

Working on your business: CRM updates, paperwork, setting up follow-ups.

■ **Red = Recharge Time**

Family, health, mental reset. Do NOT neglect this. A strong mind wins the game.

Time	Color		Activity
6:30 AM	■ Red	🧘	**Morning reset:** **Quiet time, journaling, spiritual practice**
6:45 AM	■ Red	📖	**10 minutes personal development:** **(read, watch, or listen, then APPLY)**
7:00 AM	■ Red	📝	**Write your 3 Daily Promises** **(non-negotiables for the day)**
7:30 AM	■ Grn.	🖩	**Warm Market Touchpoint: 5 texts,**

			DMs, or messages sent
8:00 AM	■ Red	🧘	Physical health: gym, walk, stretching, or movement
9:00 AM	■ Grn.	🚶	Prospecting Power Block 1:
			Social media post (1—2 posts max)
			Comment, DM, or engage with 5 new people
10:30 AM	■ Grn.	🤝	Cold Market or Event Time:
			Go APE: Appointments, Phone Calls, Events
			Start 1—2 conversations in the wild (coffee shop, gym, etc.)
12:00 PM	■ Grn.	🍽	Lunch & Learn / Networking:
			Invite new prospects or strategic partners to meet up
1:00 PM	■ Grn.	☎	Prospecting Power Block 2:
			3—5 follow-ups using "Season is the Reason" or past convo topic
			Use "If I, will you?" or takeaway posture

Time	Color		Activity
2:30 PM	Yllw.	👀	**Strategic Partner + Admin Time:**
			Reach out to 1—2 strategic connections
			Update CRM, organize leads, prep materials
4:00 PM	Yllw.	🧾	**Paperwork, Contracts, Notes:**
			Log wins, follow-up outcomes, next steps
5:00 PM	Grn.	🔄	**Bonus Prospecting: Quick wins, and 1 more call or DM**
6:00 PM	Red	👨‍👩‍👧	**Family Time: Dinner, kids, decompress**
8:00 PM	Red	💬	**15 mins of presence with spouse/ significant other**
8:30 PM	Red	🛁	**Mental break: bath, reading, silence, spiritual grounding**
9:00 PM	Red	🛏️	**Rest and reset for tomorrow**

Script Templates

Warm Market

The Direct Approach:

"Hey [Name], do you happen to know anyone that [offer]?"

The Indirect Approach:

"Hey [Name], I know you may not be looking for [offer], but is there anyone that you know that may be looking to [offer]?"

The Leverage Approach:

"Hey [Name], this is [Name of your mentor or leader]. He/she's been in the [your industry] business for [x] years. He/she's an expert in the industry. I'm happy to get you both connected."

Referral Market

Personal Introduction

"[Prospect], I would like to personally introduce you to [Referral]. [Referral] is an expert in the [XYZ Industry] and has personally helped me and my family [How they've helped you]. I know you may have someone you currently work with, but I feel a conversation with [Referral] will be worth your time."

Sphere of Influence

"Hey, [Name], I need your help. I'm looking to meet someone in [Be specific], is there any way you can make that introduction?"

Strategic Partnerships

"How can I add value to you?"

"Who is it that you are looking to meet?"

"I come across all sorts of people, if I could make one introduction for you that would help your business, who would that be?"

Collaboration Prospecting

"Hey, Joe, this is John. The reason I'm calling you is because I'm a realtor in the local market. I was wondering if you are open to collaborating and sharing business."

Specific Asks for Referrals

"[Name], do you have a best friend or family member right now that [offer]? Well, the reason I'm asking is [explain your offer], but if they don't have anybody in their corner, I'd love the opportunity to earn their business by [how you help them]. Would you mind making a personal introduction for me?"

Social Media

Search and Connect

"Hi, [potential prospect], I see we both follow [online guru]. What led you to start following them?"

Cold Market

Captain Obvious

Notice the clothing that people are wearing. Are they wearing a polo with a logo? Ask them what the logo stands for.

Are they wearing a sports team hat or shirt? Ask them if that's *their team* or are they just wearing the shirt?

The idea behind these obvious questions is just to open the conversation. It's up to you to continue the conversation. Refer back to your ABC's and use PROM (pg. 126)

Season is the Reason

"Hey [Name], did you see the game last night?"

"Hey [Name], any travel plans for the summer?"

Real estate or mortgage?

"Hey, are you in real estate or mortgages?"

If they say, "No, I'm not."

You can say, *"Oh, well you look like a realtor."*, and then continue the conversation.

If they say, "Yes, I am."

You can respond with a smile and say, *"I thought so."*, and then continue the conversation.

Other Openers

"Would you like to make more money?"

"Would you like to have a guaranteed income when you retire?"

"Do you feel you are being paid what you're worth? If not, would you be open to a conversation?"

"Would you like a more fulfilling career?"

Appendix

Coffee Shop Openers

If you're standing in line, look over your shoulder and ask someone:

"What's better to wake me up, a cappuccino or an espresso?"

They'll most likely say espresso... You say:

"Thanks for the advice. I have a long day at work."

They'll most likely ask you where you work... You say:

"I'm in [Industry]... [Tell them about your offer]."

Follow-up Openers

I Bet you Thought...

"Hey Mary, I bet you thought I forgot about you..."

Remember to smile while you say this, as they can hear your smile in your tone.

The Good News

"Hey Mary, did you hear about... [share your good news]

Door-to-Door Prospecting

This is the riskiest of all prospecting because you're literally approaching people on their private property. This is typical in the solar, real estate, and insurance industry. If you are going to go this route:

1. Wear company gear and have company identification.

2. Never go by yourself.

3. Only approach relevant leads. If you're looking for new homeowners only, try and only visit them.

4. Be as targeted as possible. Remember: *Door to door you just don't know.*

   o For example, you can go to new construction areas, so you know that everyone there is a new homeowner

   o Remember: *See's the people to seize the people*

5. Optimize your route like an Amazon driver, keeping it as efficient as possible.

6. Go to where you'll get the most success

   o For example, if you're in solar, look for middle-aged, middle-class communities, people that will be more savings-conscious

If you're in solar, your opener can sound something like this:

"Hey, happy Saturday! Are you the new homeowner? Congratulations! My name is [Name]. [Offer compliment]. We work with all the new homeowners in the area. We help people with saving money on energy costs, and I don't know if you know, but [present the problem]. We can get you guys locked in on something more affordable at a fixed rate. Could we prepare a free estimate for you guys to see how much you could save? The best part, we tell the power company the bad news, they've lost you as a customer!"

Appendix

If you're in mortgage protection, your opener can sound something like this:

"Hey, happy Saturday! Are you the new homeowner? Congratulations! I'm [Name]. First off, beautiful home. We work with all the new homeowners in the area to make sure their families are protected. Most people don't realize this, but if something unexpected happened to you, your mortgage could still be owed in full. That's why we help folks get set up with mortgage protection, so their home stays in the family no matter what.

We can put together a free estimate for you guys to see what kind of coverage makes sense. The best part? If you decide to move forward, you get peace of mind and your lender gets the news that your mortgage is now protected."

You can use AI to help you develop your door-to-door scripts. Just start with the template I gave you and have the AI modify it.

General phone call advice

The phone can seem like a thousand-pound gorilla. The best way to overcome this is to be prepared and non-attached from the outcome. Your focus is on the habit of making the calls.

- Stand up. This gives you energy.

- Smile. People can hear your smile when you speak. Your tone changes.

- Don't explain everything over the phone. Remember, an *invitation is not a presentation*

- Know your scripts and rebuttals. Have them printed out in front of you.

- Have a trainer available if you need.

- Keep it short: prospecting calls should be 2 to 3 minutes tops.

- Speak slowly and clearly.

- When following up, be a smooth operator, not pushy.

- Use fun phrases to follow-up such as:

  "I bet you thought I forgot about you!"
  "How are things?"

Closing the Prospect

When booking an appointment with a prospect, it's usually best to use the *Alternate of Choice Method.*

Here's how this works. Give them two options based on your schedule. For example:

"Joe, are you free to meet next week sometime?"

"Great, I have Wednesday or Thursday open, which ones better for you?"

Great, I can do later in the afternoon or the early morning, *which ones better for you?"*

The key phrase here is *Which one's better for you?* By asking the binary question, you are controlling the conversation.

Rebuttals for Prospecting Objections

Use the AIA Rebuttal:

Accept

Treat the objection like an egg. If you push it, it's going to crack. Receive the objection gently by accepting it. Example:

"I can appreciate that..."

"I completely understand..."

"That totally makes sense..."

This disarms the prospect.

Isolate

Use phrases such as:

"Other than [the objection]..."

"Outside of [the objection]..."

Ask

Use phrases like:

"*...Is there anything else preventing you...*"

Here's how this works in an example.

Objection: "I don't have time to meet."

Accept/Isolate/Ask: "*I totally understand! I wouldn't expect you to have that much time. Other than not having that much time, would there be any other reason why we would not be able to meet?*"

The Story Rebuttal

If you're in solar...

Objection: "Oh, I'm not interested in solar."

Rebuttal: "*Sounds like you have a story! May I ask what happened?*"

If you're in gym sales...

Objection: "No, I'm not looking for another membership."

Rebuttal: "*Sounds like you have a story! May I ask what happened?*"

If you're in network marketing...

Objection: "Oh, I tried some other stuff and it didn't work!"

Rebuttal: "*Sounds like you have a story! May I ask what happened?*"

The purpose of this rebuttal is *to disarm the prospect* and open them up for a conversation.

Other Resources

Lastly, here are some books for further reading which I wholeheartedly endorse:

Choose your Enemies Wisely by Patrick Bet-David

Go Pro by Eric Worre

Letting Go by David-Hawkins

Appendix

Three-Feet from Gold by Greg Reid and Sharon Lechter

The Richest Man in Babylon by George Clason

www.ingramcontent.com/pod-product-compliance
Lightning Source LLC
Chambersburg PA
CBHW031458120626
46545CB00005B/1657

9798992699852